# FORMULATE A WINNING PRESENTATION

## Tools for Dental and Healthcare Professionals to Compose a Talk with Impact

### By Margy Schaller

Designed by Margy Schaller & Stacy Reilly

This book is dedicated to the people who have showed up in my life and helped me become the best version of myself. I can never fully repay your gift, so this book is my way of paying it forward the best way I know how.

# TABLE OF CONTENTS

Foreword by JoAn Majors

## PART 1: Why Compose a Talk with Impact?

1: The Mystique of the Stage                           pg 13

2: What Is Your Purpose?                               pg 21

3: Speaker Stories: How and Why My                    pg 27
   Speaking Career Got Started

4: Ready, Set, Grow                                    pg 51

## PART 2: How to Build a Compelling and Memorable Presentation

5: Topic Selection                                     pg 75

6: The Cart Before the Horse: Research Your           pg 97
   Topic First

7: Never Just Write a PowerPoint                      pg 111

8: It Starts with Parts                                pg 119

9: We Are Just Wired That Way                          pg 147

10: Tying Design to Your Speaker Style,               pg 159
    Audience, and Venue

## PART 3: The Winners' Roundtable

11: Speaker Tips                                       pg 185

12: The Formula: Checklist for a Winning              pg 209
    Presentation

Resources                                             pg 213

About the Author                                      pg 216

Acknowledgements                                      pg 217

# FOREWORD

In a word, Margy Schaller is brilliant. Her process is to bring a strategic presentation system that is deliverable, teachable and at the same time honorable to a speaker's authenticity. It is evident in the many speakers she has interviewed, influenced, and included in her work here. She has a way to capture the very best of you and your information and then help you communicate this to an audience, small or large, in a way you yourself could not. It's just that simple.

This book is laid out so you can pick and choose which area of her expertise you want to focus on. However, I've made the mistake of thinking Margy was just a presentation designer. I am a member of the National Speakers Association and have heard many experts talk about how to improve our lectures. I know my stuff and am honored to be invited back to speak by many of my hosts. So, I had a notion that I knew what there was to know about my craft. I sold myself short because she is so much more than just a presentation designer, and her lessons here about assembling a lecture have helped me reexamine my techniques and make improvements.

As speakers, we get too close to our material. Imagine you need to move quickly through a maze of trees (your content), and it's so thick, it's hard to see a clear direction (your message) some days. The first thing Margy does is show you how to see the way distinctly and navigate the course with no obstructions. Her joy, talent, or gift is to lift you just high enough so that you can see it too. It's going to require some trust, and she is determined enough to earn it! As she pushes you gently toward the plane's open door, you'll be confident that she packed your parachute. Although uncomfortable at times, the process she lays out is exhilarating!

As an "inspirer" (you'll learn more about this style and others), I was stunned to realize that the more I learned from her and her book, the more obvious was my need to start over. Seriously? Start over with the hundreds of presentations I have? I am always tweaking, making small changes, and adding content, but it was daunting to think of starting over. However, to deliver what I needed to inspire greatness in my audience, every ounce of my presentation and materials needed to be in alignment. I realized my material was really heavy... too many words, too many images, just too much I didn't need to have.

This meant taking the bigger risk (redoing and getting it right) would trump my desire to be comfortable (keeping the old way or, better yet, thinking I could do it myself). My speaking and writing style is not so structured that I wouldn't be able to show up and deliver with less content preparation because I live it. As I began to immerse myself in the material and her formula, it was evident I'd never again have to guess that it was going to be fine. These systems and new awareness of my style has ensured that my material now matches the same excellence I strive to bring every time I'm on the platform. As a professional speaker who always strives to be a master of my craft, it was easy to see that I needed Margy because she is a master of hers.

The second part of her book focuses on the design elements. While I've always appreciated how brilliantly she designed my slides, I had no idea the deliberate psychology she was applying in every choice she made for me. I get a little rush every time my audience starts snapping pictures of my slides, and I know my message is hitting home in entirely new ways.

In closing, it has been three years since I first met Margy and had the privilege of having her become my content and design consultant. What she delivers in tangible goods are unmatched in my world. The quantifiable formula she delivers with multiple examples in this book are simple to understand yet challenging in many ways. Challenging because of the stretch to continue to push deep into your own content versus going wide with it. However, this is not the reason you will be compelled to return to the material and the mastery of her thought process. The reason will be in that moment that you realize you have worked, journeyed, or shared with someone who listens so intently she can complete your own thought often with more clarity than you might with your myopic view. You will find that you like yourself better in her space; it's just an ability she has.

For someone in my work space to become so committed to my success has been mind-blowing and may just be her greatest value. Use this formula, work this plan, trust her lead, and your audiences, small or large, will thank you and be influenced beyond your imagination by your signature delivery! Enjoy the journey!

See you on the road,

JoAn Majors
Professional Speaker, Published Author and Founder of
The ProPractice Online Learning Platform

# WHY COMPOSE A TALK WITH IMPACT?

# CHAPTER 1
## THE MYSTIQUE OF THE STAGE

Ever since I was a little girl, I've had a love affair with the stage. It started when I was six years old and had a solo part in the first-grade play. I felt a magical connection with the audience. They wanted me to do well and I felt their support. BAM! I was hooked. I continued in theater all the way through high school and college. I always volunteered to go first in my speech classes and watched the instructors with envy when I attended those standard corporate training courses early in my working life. However, it took me 10 years to realize that training and education was the field I wanted to pursue.

During those 10 years, I had two young children and didn't want to try to combine motherhood with a job that would require full-time travel, so I enrolled and completed the highest level of training for instructional designers at the Langevin Learning Centers (the leading professional certification center for trainers). The course work covered everything from Training Needs Analysis to Adult Learning Theory and from How to Influence People to Writing Training with Impact. I launched my new career as an instructional designer by writing training courses for a consulting firm who served high-tech companies. I was able to do on-site needs analysis, write and then conduct pilot courses, and, finally, turn over the end product to trainers who used that content all over the world.

September 11, 2001. Companies across the country hunkered down. They feared economic disaster and slashed every budget they thought was disposable, including training budgets. Suddenly, I had to reinvent myself again.

In 2002, I got a position at a drug discovery company, where I located and recruited university thought leaders to consult for us. Based upon my ability to connect with these experts in the healthcare arena, I was recruited to establish a Speaker's Bureau for a gastroenterology diagnostics company. My next position came from a dental implant company who wanted to elevate their continuing education offerings to be more than just an arm of the sales team. During this phase of my career, I discovered a real connection to dental and healthcare speakers. These clinicians are passionate about what they do, are incredibly bright and articulate, and most of all, want to share their knowledge with others.

While these positions brought me back to the speaking and training field, I found that I was too far on the periphery, and I longed for more. In May 2013, with my youngest off to college, I had the opportunity to launch my own company. I started Laser Pointer to bring together my love and passion for speakers with my knowledge of how adults learn. I love helping dental and healthcare speakers formulate their winning presentations.

Although most of my clients are nationally recognized keynote speakers, some are brand new speakers who are eager for expert guidance and for a system that they can follow to create lectures or training courses. What I have come to realize is that everyone wants to be that captivating speaker, and while many of my successful clients have intuitively figured some of this out, all of them are grateful for the little tweak that can help them go from good to great to profound. For others, time is the hurdle to taking things to the next level. Many of my clients already give up too much of their personal time to be a speaker and are thrilled that I can give them back some of their family time, or time in nature, or time to reconnect with themselves.

So who is this book for?

This book is for you, the speaker. Whether you are new or experienced, hopefully you will find nuggets you can use on how to write a compelling talk, design presentations for new and existing talks, and succeed in the speaking business. I will leave the podium skills training to others and focus solely on the preparation stage of this process.

## The Expert

The expert is the speaker at the top of their game. Some started back when they had to assemble their slides in 35mm slide carousels and carefully carry them onto the airplane. Others in this group have risen quickly through the ranks based upon their talent and subject matter. These in-demand speakers typically give some variation of the same talk repeatedly over the course of a couple of years and know their material inside and out.

The problem is often twofold. First, they don't have the time or perhaps the knowledge to design anything other than the most expedient slides, and second, they change their slides on the fly all the time.

For these speakers, I focus on giving their core slide deck a professional polish. This may involve a custom background and unified and stylish fonts. In addition, I work on de-cluttering text-heavy slides and substituting images or icons in these established slide decks wherever possible.

## The Rising Star

The rising star is someone who has been speaking locally for some time and has been booked for a major platform. These speakers want to take it up a notch and call me for help.

The problem is that they really want to make a great impression but don't know how.

We spend time upfront talking about the purpose and takeaways. I often say that if the speaker doesn't know what they want people to remember, neither will the audience. From there, we get into structure and design elements to drive home the message.

The outcome? Speakers often tell me that they feel more confident and able to communicate their message, and the audience is more engaged.

## The Novice

I have worked with a number of people who are early in their speaking career. They have some expertise or ideas to share but are not necessarily sure how to get started.

The problem is that they are often overwhelmed and don't know how to get from here to there.

I work with these clients from soup to nuts—from teaching them how to write their talk to designing their slides, and to even helping them develop collateral materials such as handouts.

The outcome? These speakers have catapulted their speaking career right out of the gate by using a professional to minimize their learning curve and maximize their opportunities.

Ernest Hemingway said, "There is nothing noble in being superior to your fellow man; true nobility is being superior to your former self." The platform of being a speaker is an honor and a privilege, so wherever you fall on the spectrum of speaker, what are you doing to raise your own bar?

As a speaker myself, I am grateful every time I get in front of an audience and commit to that unspoken agreement that we will share something special together, something that will only happen during this moment. To me, that is the mystique of the stage, and I am equally grateful for the opportunity to help other speakers on their quest to become their very best selves—to help share the mystique. I am in my happy place with all I get to do today.

Finally, I want to acknowledge that much of the expertise and knowledge I have gained is an accumulation of wisdom from some exceptional speakers who I have worked with over the years. Some of those speakers allowed me to interview them for this book, and I will share some of their stories and tips with you in hopes of shortening your learning curve.

# CHAPTER 2
## WHAT IS YOUR PURPOSE?

Success is more than being an expert at something; it is also knowing yourself well enough to set yourself up for success. In working with speakers for over 16 years, I have observed that the really good ones know why they are on the podium. It comes down to purpose.

Speaking on a regular basis is a calling. It doesn't typically result in a huge financial gain, it is physically demanding, and it takes us away from family and our day job. Then, why do so many people want to be speakers? It's because we are willing to go to great lengths to deliver on some promise.

I believe that if we have clarity about what that promise is, then writing, assembling, designing, and delivering our presentation will be more fun and more successful. I have observed that these promises or purposes for speaking fall into four categories, and I have named four Speaker Styles<sup>SM</sup> representative of those purposes that we will discuss throughout this book.

## PURPOSE #1

You have a product or service that you believe makes people's lives better.

## PURPOSE #2

You have achieved excellence in your field and you feel driven to share your discoveries with others.

## PURPOSE #3

You had really good mentors and now want to pay it forward.

## PURPOSE #4:

You have new data, a new gold standard, or a new law that you believe the world needs to know in order to succeed.

# THE 4 SPEAKER STYLES<sup>SM</sup>

### Speaker Style #1: Recruiter
Most consultants and sales people are recruiters. These speakers believe that their product or service will help the audience to enjoy an easier, more efficient, more profitable way of doing their job.

### Speaker Style #2: Inspirer
These speakers are typically at the very top of their field and are the keynote speakers brought in to WOW us at major meetings. They know (and we know) that most people can't achieve the results they get, but in delivering their lecture, they hope people will stretch themselves further than they have before.

### Speaker Style #3: Trainer
These are the clinicians and consultants who teach people how to actually do what they do. They work tirelessly going from group to group, breaking down a process or procedure into a step-by-step methodology, and helping their peers gain competency. They gain great satisfaction from seeing the lightbulb come on for their attendees.

### Speaker Style #4: Informer
Often, these are people who have been burned by lack of information sometime in their past or whose subject matter is complex but needs to be accessible (CPA, HR, Insurance Coding, etc.). They have a great passion for teaching people the rules and regulations that keep changing in their field.

It gets tricky when we try to figure out what we are. Most people at first glance say that they are a blend of all the speaker styles. I would argue that we should pick one and knock that one out of the ballpark. Here is an example of how to zero in on your primary purpose and speaker style:

Say you just got finished publishing a new book on tidying up your desk. You might say that you are a recruiter because you want others to buy your book, or you could be a trainer because you teach people how to clean their desks. However, those outcomes are not tied to our purpose or our beliefs. Our beliefs might be that a quiet mind gives us space to create great thoughts. A clean desk is just the <u>what</u> and our method in the book is just the <u>how</u>. If our talk is focused on the end game of being our best selves, our WHY actually makes us an inspirer.

With clarity about your own style, you can focus your energy on creating a lecture that plays to your strengths. You can identify your own strengths and weaknesses as well as your opportunities for growth. You can use your primary speaker style to frame your content, design your slides, and select the type of speaking opportunities you want.

Later in this book, we will take a deeper look at how the audience's expectations often impact which type of speaker will succeed. As in this case study, a very successful speaker of one type can struggle in an audience of a different type. If you have a very distinct style, only accept speaking invitations where you are likely to be well received. Remember, your reputation is only as good as your last gig!

## Case Example

A humble restorative general dentist was a sole practitioner for over 40 years and knew how to MacGyver anything. He had seen it all and could come up with solutions for the craziest complications. This made him an extremely popular speaker for local study clubs and referral group programs. He was in such demand that he spoke almost every week and was booked 9–12 months in advance. He was so well regarded that a corporate sponsor eagerly supported his honorarium for many of his lectures. One year, this corporate sponsor invited him to speak at a national trade show's Corporate Forum... where he fell absolutely flat. What happened? His speaking style was to walk among the audience, tell his personal stories, and ask questions, and his presentation was a hodgepodge of old case images and steps typed out in white font on a blue background. At the Corporate Forum, he was stuck behind a podium, and he disappointed the audience because they were expecting great images and new techniques. He was a true teacher, and this venue called for an inspirer.

The saddest part was that neither he nor the corporate sponsor knew what went wrong, and both came to the erroneous conclusion that he was not as good a speaker as he had once been. His reputation with the sponsor was never the same.

# CHAPTER 3
## SPEAKER STORIES: HOW AND WHY MY SPEAKING CAREER GOT STARTED

When people find out what I do, many of them say that they have always wanted to be a speaker but didn't know how to go about it. What I have learned is that there are as many different ways people have started their speaking career as there are speakers. Here are some stories from professional speakers about how they got their start.

I had never necessarily aspired to be a speaker, it just kind of happened. I have always been an outgoing-type person, but I never planned when I started my practice that going out and speaking or teaching would be a significant part of what I was doing in my career.

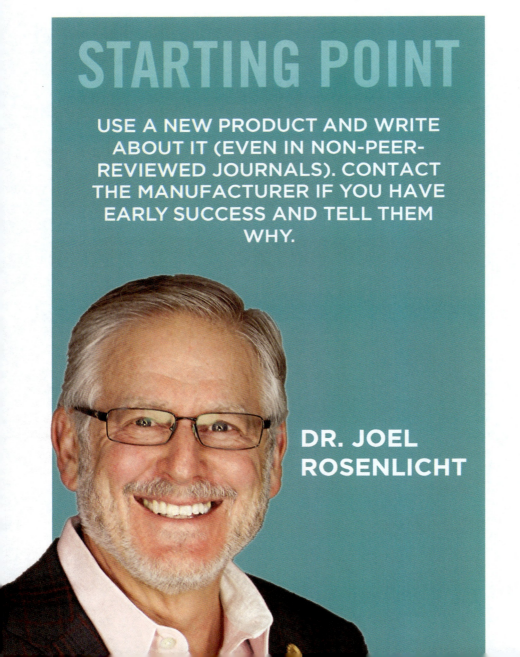

STARTING POINT

USE A NEW PRODUCT AND WRITE ABOUT IT (EVEN IN NON-PEER-REVIEWED JOURNALS). CONTACT THE MANUFACTURER IF YOU HAVE EARLY SUCCESS AND TELL THEM WHY.

DR. JOEL ROSENLICHT

It was in the early 1980s, when implants were just starting to get popular, and there were just a couple of companies. One implant I liked, the TPS screw (one-stage, one-piece implant) was from the International Team of Implantologists (ITI) from Switzerland. It was marketed at that time by an orthopedic company called Synthes, and I knew of them from some of the orthonapic surgery I had been doing (bone plates and screws for fractures). They saw early on that I was using the system because I had written some articles for some "throwaway" journals. They contacted me and asked me to come talk about my experience with this implant at their home office where they put on programs. What was fortunate for me was that they also had invited another speaker, somebody who I had only known about by reputation, Dr. Charles Babbish. At first I was very intimidated, but I enjoyed the experience very much.

This led to our lecturing together all around the US for a period of months. I used 35mm slides and then ad-libbed my presentation. These were all-day or weekend presentations (I had five to seven carousels I carried around), so it was crude compared to today. I enjoyed the travel, the chance to meet different dentists, and I think I truly enjoyed the opportunity to teach. Audiences were smaller, with relatively enthusiastic attendees, so that made it more personal and intimate, with more Q&A. I was able to develop camaraderie and trust, and in those early years, we carried on communication with our attendees way beyond the lectures that we gave. They would call and write afterwards, and we would keep the dialogue going, so I met some really smart professionals from all around the country.

I was a dentist for 23 years. I was at the American Dental Association meeting in San Francisco when I got a call from my wife. She was still at home and explained to me that our custodian had called to say that the FBI was at our office, had battered down the door, and was taking all of our records out. It was disconcerting to say the

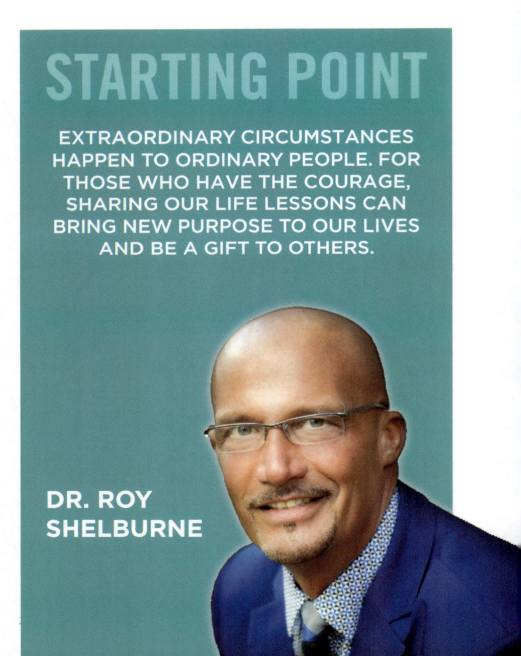

# STARTING POINT

**EXTRAORDINARY CIRCUMSTANCES HAPPEN TO ORDINARY PEOPLE. FOR THOSE WHO HAVE THE COURAGE, SHARING OUR LIFE LESSONS CAN BRING NEW PURPOSE TO OUR LIVES AND BE A GIFT TO OTHERS.**

## DR. ROY SHELBURNE

least, but that set into motion a change in my life that ultimately led to my speaking career.

While I was being investigated for healthcare fraud, I learned a lot about what needs to be done to protect and defend a practice, what I should have done that I didn't do, and things that I did do that I shouldn't have done. Prior to this, I never had the opportunity to understand #1, the gravity of what could happen, and #2, the definition of "intent to defraud." I thought if I ever made a mistake or was paid anything unintentionally that I could return it and that would be that. I was never given that option. Actually, the legal definition of "intent to defraud" is that if you knew you were committing fraud, or you SHOULD have known (which means continuing to do the same thing the same way without having systems in place to identify and correct those errors), you are guilty of intent to defraud.

So, I was investigated for three years, indicted, and then a year and half later I went to trial, where I was eventually found guilty of intent to defraud. Shortly before surrendering myself to go to prison, I got a call from Linda Miles, a great friend and visionary. She explained that not only did she speak and consult for dental practices, she also had an organization that taught individuals who were interested in speaking or consulting in the dental industry to be better equipped to do this. She told me, "Roy, you are going to be a speaker." I laughed and said, "Linda, do you have any idea what happened and what is going on?" and she said, "Yes, and that is exactly why you not only need to tell your story, but you <u>have</u> to tell your story." I thought about this the whole term I was in prison (19 months, plus 2 months in a halfway house).

It took a while to be able to come to grips with what had happened to me and even longer to become okay with it. I believe everything happens for a reason, and so now the tagline on my email says, "A bend in the road is only the end of the road if you fail to make the turn." What happened to me is probably the worst thing that could ever happen to a professional, but it doesn't hold a candle to losing a loved one, so I try to put things in perspective.

Literally the day after I was released from custody, Linda arranged for me to go to the Speaking Consulting Network (SCN) meeting, and I found myself on a flight to Anaheim so that I could learn how to be a speaker. While I enjoyed the meeting, I was thinking, "Well, that is great for them, but I'm a convicted felon in a very conservative industry, and I don't have a dental license anymore." I had just been offered a job working in a dental lab for not much over minimum wage. I had not thought it was possible to support myself as a speaker, even for someone at the top of their game, never mind someone who had my history and my experience. I never thought it was possible—no, I didn't. It was the furthest thing from my mind. I mean, I enjoyed the meeting, but I thought this was something that was just not going to happen.

Six months later (November 2010), I was contacted by a specialist in Newport News, Virginia, who wanted me to come speak for his referring doctor appreciation event. I asked him if he knew who I was and what had happened to me, and he assured me that he had followed the story on Dental Town (a large thread on that website was about my case).

I put together a slide set that highlighted the issues that I learned from my practice errors to share with that audience so that they could be better equipped to meet any challenge. It was too late for me, but I wanted to do what I could to help offices out there understand the danger of ignorance and of not being prepared. You have an opportunity to protect and defend your practice, and although it's not glamorous and it doesn't generate a whole lot of revenue, it is vitally important if you are ever challenged. And it's not just from the government, it's from insurance agencies, it's from malpractice claims, it's from dental board complaints...there are a number of things we aren't even aware of because these dangers didn't exist 15–20 years ago, but they've become very real and apparent, and it is happening with greater frequency, and we need to be able to address these issues.

I was a little trepidatious beforehand, so an old college friend came and taped it with a video camera for me to review afterwards. It turned out that the feedback after the presentation was tremendous, both from the doctor who invited me as well as from those who attended. Early on I had that brief exposure to what I should do at SCN, so I had developed a brief evaluation form to get feedback to make changes going forward. My college friend's comment was "I had no idea you could do something like this; that was REALLY good!"

# STARTING POINT

START SPEAKING LOCALLY, WHETHER AT YOUR OWN STUDY CLUB OR FOR LOCAL SOCIETIES. OFFER TO SWAP SPEAKING ENGAGEMENTS WITH COLLEAGUES FOR EACH OTHER'S GROUPS (THEY WILL BE GLAD TO GET FREE SPEAKERS!). IF YOU ARE A SPECIALIST, SPEAK FOR YOUR REFERRAL BASE AND DO PATIENT EDUCATION SEMINARS AS OFTEN AS POSSIBLE, AND WHEN THAT INVITATION COMES FOR A BIG PROGRAM, DON'T LET FEAR STOP YOU FROM JUMPING INTO THE DEEP END.

**DR. TOM KEPIC**

Even from a young age I've never been shy speaking in front of people. Early on in my periodontal practice, I presented an occasional one-two hour lecture for my local general dentists or hygiene / dental assisting groups.  But I had no aspirations of being a professional speaker.

About twenty-five years ago, I was asked by a hygienist who previously worked in our practice to give a full day program (two separate three hour lectures) for a Dental Hygiene Society in Napa, CA. I freaked out because I didn't have anyone to help me prepare my lectures.

The lecture was in a winery in downtown Napa.  I remember the floor being very cold and damp. The chill went all the way through me!  I felt great once it was over but it was overwhelming to lecture an entire day.  Once I did it and got positive reviews, it gave me confidence that I could lecture again.

It became common for groups to ask me to lecture, locally, nationally, and internationally. I've since lectured in ten dental schools.  It has enhanced my reputation and given me credibility.

# STARTING POINT

IF YOU FIND YOU HAVE A GIFT FOR HELPING OTHERS IMPROVE IN THEIR PROFESSION, TRY SPEAKING AT A SMALL VENUE. SOME PEOPLE DISCOVER THEY HAVE A CALLING AS A SPEAKER, AND IF THIS IS YOU, SPEND THE TIME, EFFORT, AND MONEY TO HONE YOUR SKILLS. SURROUND YOURSELF WITH GREAT MENTORS AND ATTEND SPEAKER CONFERENCES SUCH AS SCN AND THE NSA.

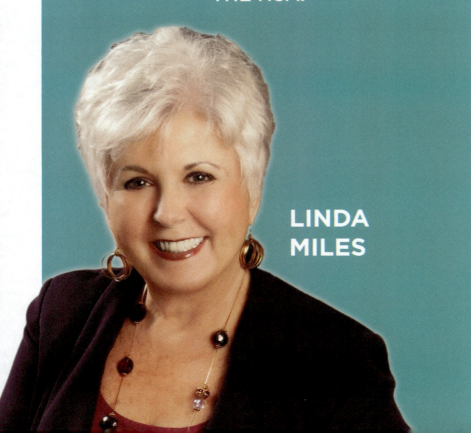

LINDA
MILES

I was a dental assistant for 14 years, and during that time, my boss created these little pre- and post-clinical explanation cards with pictures on them to save time and to be more effective in explaining things to patients. The result was that it saved our doctors seven minutes per patient, which allowed them to do more dentistry.

I then changed jobs in 1970 and was hired as the first employee of a new practice. I had been an endodontic assistant for a methodical doctor, and this new doctor was a very fast-moving GP, and it showed up quickly that I was very rusty. However, instead of firing me, he asked me to go up front and run the practice. I agreed and asked him to teach me how to do this. He didn't know either, so he sent me to meetings to learn, and the more I learned, the more I realized that there were weaknesses in the office management system! So, I started creating things: the very first collection system, the very first inventory control system, a pending appointment system (to address the greatest weakness of patients saying "I'll call back later for an appointment").

My boss was so impressed with all of this that he started telling all his buddies about it, and then they wanted to know what I did with my day off. As a result, I started working with four practices on my day off in Richmond, VA. I spent four hours each at two practices one week and then went to the other two practices the next week. And they started asking me how much did I charge for my consulting, and I thought, "Oh my gosh, that's a good word, I might use that someday in the future." I said, "I don't know how well these ideas might work for you, so just send me a check in 30 days for whatever you think my time was worth." I was helping their teams with telephone techniques, greeting patients warmly, chairside communication, marketing, scheduling, reducing broken and lost appointments, inventory systems... basically everything I had created for our office, I shared with these other doctors. Well, at the time I was making $185/$200 week, and these doctors sent me a check for $400 for four hours! I said, "Now, this is fun, and I have to find a name for it!"

One of those four doctors said, "Linda, we have absolutely enjoyed having you in our office these past few months; more importantly, we are producing double the amount we used to because of your scheduling concepts. We all love to come to work now because we are organized, productive, and can see a bright future. Why don't you hold a seminar and invite lots of people?" My response to that was, "Do you really think I can talk all day?" and he said, "YES!"

As it turned out, that first seminar was horrible! I had 36 pages written out on a legal pad, and I was so scared, and I was not a speaker, and I literally read those pages to those poor people for six hours. I was the worst speaker on planet earth.

Nevertheless, I was determined to get better, so I borrowed $500 from the bank to make my first marketing brochure. It was brown-on-brown using a passport picture, and it was pitiful. It was so pitiful that I think 36 people came to my first public seminar in Richmond, Virginia. After my disastrous first program, I spent four months writing and preparing for that seminar. Now, it would take me 40 minutes to do the same thing.

I continued doing that part-time from 1978–1980, and when my husband was transferred to Virginia Beach for the Air Force, I decided that I would not take a job in dentistry—I would just get this business going. It was really tough because when you move, nobody knows you, and of course, this was before the Internet where you could spread the word anywhere. So, I just started out holding little local public seminars; I called them my "Beach Seminars."

After a while, I was able to expand, and on a Friday and Saturday, I would go to two cities for two programs; I went to Nashville and Memphis, Philadelphia and Pittsburgh, Charlotte and Raleigh. There might have been 35–40 people per seminar, so I was not losing money, but I was not making money.

Thank goodness, my husband was out on a 15-month assignment, so I had time to work on this business. I worked during the school day, then put my 11- and 15-year-old kids to bed, and then worked some more until two or three a.m. I decided to go visit my husband (near Seattle, WA), and deliver two seminars while I was out there. I checked in early to one of the hotels, and the bellman said, "Did you know that there is a seminar being held here? It is down in the basement and there are about 300 people in attendance." I said, "Oh really, I'm a speaker too" (I had only done about four seminars at this time), so I thought, "Okay, I'll just go down there and check it out." I ran downstairs, and the ticket to get in turned out to be the best $35 I've ever spent in my life! This was 1979, and I happened to be in a navy-blue suit, a raspberry-colored blouse, and navy-blue heels, and I look around and I was sitting with 300 lumberjacks! The two speakers turned out to be Mark Victor Hansen (who was as poor as I was at the time, but is one of the two authors of Chicken Soup for the Soul, markvictorhansen.com), and Jim Tunney (an NFL referee, www.jimtunney.com), and they were just baby speakers at the time.

During the dinner break, I was sitting by myself at the restaurant, and Mark Victor Hansen came running over and said, "You're in our seminar, aren't you?" and I know I stuck out like a sore thumb among all these lumberjacks, and he said, "Come and join the head table." As I sat there with 12 others, I was mesmerized when they told me there was actually a group called the National Speaker's Association (NSA) and they said that I should join. Now, I did not have the money to go to that NSA meeting in Chicago, but they said that I had to find a way to go, be it beg, steal, rob a 7-11, whatever, I had to go.

Well, my dad ended up lending me the money, and I went. There was Zig Ziglar and Jim and Naomi Rhodes, and there were so many famous people, all the superstars. After that conference, I was hooked on being a speaker!

# STARTING POINT

MANY PEOPLE SPEAK TO THEIR LOCAL REFERRAL NETWORK AND AT LOCAL ASSOCIATIONS AS A WAY TO ESTABLISH THEMSELVES AS EXPERTS. THIS CAN BE A MEANS TO AN END FOR BUILDING A REFERRAL BASE OR FOR CREATING A LAUNCHING PAD TO A LARGER SPEAKING CAREER.

**DR. TIM SILEGY**

I suppose I've always kind of had a knack for public speaking. I remember taking a speech class in college. I chose to present a lecture on Chymopapain, a papaya-derived enzyme used to treat herniated discs non-surgically. Few of my fellow students in the class had a science background, so my task was to figure out a way to help them first understand an anatomical problem, and then understand how this innovative concept was being used to treat it. Not only did I receive an "A" on the lecture, but numerous students complimented me on my performance. This was when I first realized I had the ability to take fairly complex things and bundle them into a package that even a novice could understand.

When I finished my oral surgery training, I realized that one of the ways I could establish my credibility and reputation was by lecturing to potential referrals. I started study clubs and gave numerous Lunch and Learns on topics they would find relevant. As a resident, every Wednesday we had to present a case, defend our treatment choices, and answer questions, so these talks were kind of a natural progression.

I have always made a point to document my cases. As my collection of cases grew, I had the material and experience necessary to lecture to more diverse groups.

# STARTING POINT

SPEAKING AND TEACHING ARE OFTEN INTERTWINED. SPEAKING FOR A REGULAR GROUP CAN BE A LAUNCHING PAD FOR BOTH FACULTY AND PAID SPEAKING POSITIONS.

**DR. STEPHEN SADOWSKY**

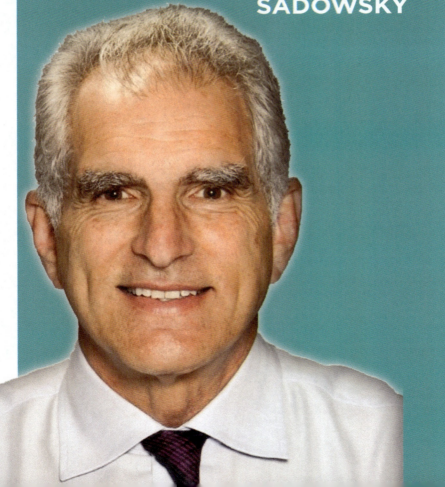

I went to postgraduate school at USC for prosthodontics after my dental school experience and nine years of private practice, and after that two-year postgraduate program, I became enamored by the Odontic Seminar, which was an ongoing prosthodontic group at USC and was part of the reason why I went to grad school.
I always knew I wanted to go into speaking and be a teacher (I come from a line of teachers), and I found out later that this is how I learn best. It's very stimulating, and I'm always getting to improve. So, after graduation, I became part of their part-time faculty for 25 years, and that became my training ground to develop my speaking skills. I spoke once a month on various topics that I developed a presentation for that was akin to the overall topic that we wanted to develop.

This seminar met 10 months a year, and the participants came year after year, so we had to adapt the material along the way to keep it current and make it applicable for them. The good news is that I had a chance to have great relationships with the attendees and get good feedback while also learning from my mentors.

I don't remember the very first time I spoke, but I can tell you that it was not the only time that I was nervous! It took many, many experiences before something changed... and then I learned an axiom for myself, and that was (1) If I was very prepared, I was relaxed, and (2) If I had a creative angle that was unique, then I was excited to share it (rather than nervous). Those two things allowed me to get into my zone or my own way of feeling at home.

# STARTING POINT

CONNECTIONS ARE MADE EVERY DAY, AND YOU NEVER KNOW WHERE THAT WILL LEAD YOU. IF YOU ARE OPEN TO POSSIBILITIES AND SUGGESTIONS, DOORS CAN OPEN FOR YOU!

**DR. TANYA BROWN**

The first time I remember speaking to a large dental group was at The Dawson Academy Alumni Meeting in 2004. I was asked to present through Buddy Shafer, co-owner of Bay View Dental Laboratory who I met when I attended the Dawson Academy. They asked me to speak on Team Development and Practice Management.

Even as a kid, I can remember being called on in class to stand up and speak first since my last name started with an "A". I have always enjoyed relating to people... so as I started speaking and people were giving me feedback like, "Hey, you really have a gift". Then I decided I was going to learn and grow so I could share with others, and one thing led to another!

In 2009, I joined SCN, The Speaking Consulting Network and that is where my speaking and consulting career launched to the next level. Linda Miles started SCN to help speakers and consultants come together and elevate each other. From there I joined the National Speakers Association, which opened my eyes to the possibility of speaking as a career.

# STARTING POINT

## START SMALL AND FIND YOUR NICHE. THEN SUBMIT ARTICLES TO GAIN CREDIBILITY.

**RACHEL WALL, RDH**

I got my start in consulting working alongside a well-established dental consultant, so my first presenting encounters were in the dental office. I then progressed to presentations for local hygiene component meetings, and my first big speaking engagement was at RDH Under One Roof. In fact, when I was presenting recently in California a few attendees said, "Oh, we saw you speak at RDH Under One Roof in 2005!" and I said, "Oh, I'm so sorry..." I will never forget that experience. I was a brand new speaker, and I was presenting in a huge ballroom that would seat 400–500 people. I probably had 50 attendees, and I was presenting at the same time as a very popular speaker. They were in a smaller room, and I was in this beautiful, but very large room. I will never forget my host (who was introducing me), Dianne Watterson. Dianne has been an icon in dental hygiene for many years and is so much more experienced than me. She was very kind, and at the end of it, she said in her own Southern way, "Well that was a big piece of meat to chew for the first time out!" She was right! I don't think I did well in that speech... It was a three-hour talk, and I think I ended about 45 minutes early. Fortunately, I was asked to speak at RDH again several years later and had a great experience. I didn't completely blow my entire speaking career, but it was a bit of a rough start.

The reason that I was first asked to speak at RDH-UOR was that I had written for their magazine a couple of times. It is my understanding that the publishers like to have article contributors also be speakers so that the readers can meet the contributors when they come to the meeting.

# CHAPTER 4
## READY, SET, GROW

### What Impact Do You Want to Make?

As you can see, many of these speakers had no thought or plan to become a speaker. In fact, every speaker I've met started by speaking locally, whether it was in residency or for a study club or for their referral network. For most, once they had a taste of the rush of speaking, they sought out more. But what does "more" look like?

Each speaker's definition of winning varies. The primary driver is their underlying purpose. These drivers in turn set the goalposts for what success looks like to them.

### DR. TIM SILEGY

First, I think it's important to figure out why you want to be a speaker and then as objectively as possible determine whether you are any good at it. If you have a knack for it, it's worth pursuing. I get a certain enjoyment being in front of a group and being effective in helping teach them something. If you are a great orator, then you can move, touch, and inspire people, but if the material isn't good, it's not going to accomplish much.

## LINDA MILES

Seventy percent of the big ideas that I created in the past 36 years failed miserably, despite hours and hours of my time and often lots of money invested. However, 30 percent of those big ideas worked much better than I ever dreamed they would, so you just keep trying new things or different pathways or set it aside and come back later to see if it looks different. My theory has always been that even a blind pig finds an ear of corn one day because it just keeps rooting around, so keep trying to find the magic that will carry that big idea.

## DR. TANYA BROWN

In my 25 plus years in dentistry, I have come across too many Dentists who have advanced degrees, significant debt, dental offices full of the latest technology, and yet they truly struggle with helping patients say "YES" to their treatment recommendations. So, as a practicing dentist and practice management consultant, I believe helping patients say "Yes", has a significant impact on your patients, team, and practice. I'm thrilled when people tell me stories about they tried something I shared and how well it worked in their practice. I want to be more than just "successful", I want to have a significant impact on dentists, dental teams, patients, and practices & have them leave my programs inspired and ready to implement what they learned.

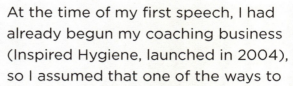

## RACHEL WALL, RHD

At the time of my first speech, I had already begun my coaching business (Inspired Hygiene, launched in 2004), so I assumed that one of the ways to build a consulting business was through speaking. That was something that I wanted to bring into my profession.

## Choose your audience to align with your purpose

 If you have a product/service that you believe will benefit your audience (recruiter), your geographic reach will be dependent on your product/service reach. In addition, your target audience should be limited to your ideal customer.

 If you are a professional who excels in your field and you want to move the audience forward (inspirer), your goal should be to provide main podium keynote lectures at large society/association meetings.

 Workshops, study clubs, and training centers are the ideal venue for you if you are the teacher (you have a love for your profession and want to pay it forward).

 Similarly, as with the recruiter, the informer (you have new information that the audience needs to be successful) should seek out venues that align with those that need this information.

## Where Are You Going?

Once you have greater clarity on the impact you want to make and what winning looks like, you also need to determine what type of travel you are willing to do. Here are some speaking engagement scenarios to bear in mind when developing the type of speaking career you desire:

**Occasional speaker within driving distance of home.**

**Regular speaker for study clubs and referral groups.**

**National/international speaker on main podiums.**

**Speaking designed to grow your business.**

## Occasional speaker within driving distance of home

There is an adage that the best speaker is from anywhere but here. As such, you will rarely be able to get much traction speaking in your hometown. Rather, look up who is in charge of organizations within your chosen geographic radius and then use every opportunity to network with them or their peers. (State association meetings are a great place to start). Once you have spoken for someone (and it went well), ask them if they would be willing to recommend you for other speaking engagements.

For this to work, you probably want to become an expert on a topic that has regular updates. You can build a reputation as the go-to person for new developments with a product, changes in the way something is handled in the office, or bringing meaning to emerging research on a topic.

## Study club and referral group speaker

The fastest way to launch this type of speaking career is by partnering with a company who has a product you believe in. Call them (or your sales rep) and ask how to get on their speaker's bureau. Be easy to work with and agreeable to their honorarium structure. Volume and visibility will pay off in the long run!

### DR. TIM SILEGY

When I first started using Zimmer implants, I had a fair amount of success with it. My sales rep introduced me to the VP of Sales, who then invited me to give a talk to the entire sales team on my experience with their implants. I spoke on my thought process as an oral surgeon as well as on my business philosophy for using implants. That was my first experience speaking for Zimmer, and once the sales team knew me, I started being invited to speak at more and more events.

You can also go the traditional route of networking and building your speaking through reputation building, but the process of getting known is a slower one unless you have a unique value proposition.

The most valuable speaker in this group is the teacher. If you do an effective job of teaching or transmitting a valuable skill or message to a group, they will share their enthusiasm for your program with others, and you will be a hot commodity!

I much prefer smaller groups (20–30 people) because I'm not one to stand behind a podium. I would rather go up to my audience and interact with them. It's more difficult for me to be effective speaking to a large group because, for one, it's harder to tell who is in that group. With a small group, I can have everyone introduce themselves! Keynote programs are typically more programed and less extemporaneous, making it more difficult to connect with your audience.

## DR. STEVEN SADOWSKY

I sold my practice in 2008 because I wanted to go into full-time teaching at a university. Outside speaking was a natural outgrowth because we are doing things that are on the cutting edge, which translated well with that audience. I did do some things to open them further by establishing a relationship with industry.

## National/international speaker on main podiums

Most main podium speakers are either published researchers or incredibly talented at their craft. If this is your eventual aspiration, you would be well served to identify a mentor who you can learn from and then figure out how you can help them. Top thought leaders are so jammed for time that they are grateful for help, and in turn, may be willing to bring you into their network. These national level programs also typically have scouts that go from meeting to meeting looking for a good match for their program. Once you have been invited to a larger meeting and feel confident about your skills, invite scouts to attend your program.

Main podium speakers are inspirers, leading and pushing the dental community to stretch further than they thought possible. If you are an early adopter of new technologies or products or you create solutions to problems that can be duplicated by others, you might be a good main podium candidate.

## LINDA MILES

I set a 10-year goal for myself to be a speaker at Hinman. As luck would have it, there was someone at one of my Atlanta seminars who invited me back to give an all-day talk at his study club. At that meeting, there was someone from Hinman, and he invited me to speak there, so I was actually invited to speak at Hinman by my third year! Lots of other scouts were there and saw me, and I was sort of a novelty at that time (an administrative person teaching dentists and team members), teaching how to better communicate, become organized, set up systems, and have good customer service.

## DR. ROY SHELBURNE

One of the things that I deliberately do is to be as visible as possible. Large meetings provide refreshment areas for meeting planners, scout, speakers, and the press... so whenever that room is open and I'm not speaking, I am in there trying to meet as many people as I possibly can and sharing my story when appropriate, and I've gotten a number of speaking engagements doing that. They may not have targeted my presentation when just flipping through the book, but after talking with me, they will often come to hear my lecture and see how it might work for their meeting.

## Speaking designed to grow your business

If you are using speaking as a way to grow your own business, you are in luck! There are limitless ways that this is being done:

Commercial Programs:
- Invite the attendees to a function and tell them about your product (dinners, all-day seminars, webinars, etc.).
- Piggyback with vendors who have the same target customer. If each of you invites your existing customers (where there is trust already built), you can promote each other and grow all of your businesses.
- Teach a group or practice at an on-site program.
- Sponsor a speaker and have a chance to present your topic during a meal or break.

Non-Commercial Programs:
- Due to your expertise on a topic, you might be invited to speak at a CE program. The expectation is that you will not promote your business, but the afterglow is a strong sales tactic.
- Lectures at your own associations help you establish your reputation as a thought leader.

## RACHEL WALL, RHD

I had an assumption that I could grow my business through speaking. What I have found is that I have to be very strategic about my desired outcome of a speech. If my goal is to gain leads for coaching clients, the message and desired audience may be different than it would be if I'm going to be a paid speaker at a CE conference.

I joined SCN shortly before that initial RDH-UOR speech. Then I attended Katherine Eitel-Belt's Lioness Learning (www.lionesslearning.com) training, which has been a complete game-changer. I'm still on a steep learning curve. Because of the consulting and coaching piece, I have gotten very comfortable with going into a practice and leading a workshop or leading a training. That was my comfort zone. Doing a big lecture was not in my comfort zone, and it was not something I enjoyed until very recently. My speaking colleagues had told me that repetition and doing a lot of speaking in a short period of time would allow me to hone my skills and be more comfortable presenting to large audiences. They were right. In years past, it would be six months between large lectures, so it was almost like I had to go through and refresh myself every time. Now it flows, and I feel more confident since I've been doing it more frequently.

**LINDA MILES**

When it came to the end of a shorter presentation, I would ask three thought-provoking questions, look at my watch and say, "Gee, my time is up. How I wish I had a full day to spend with you and your entire team to show you how easy it is to manage a practice when everyone understands the doctor's vision and is on board and you have systems in place and you can double your practice." Well after that, nine out of 10 practices wanted to book me for the all-day seminar!

That was the start of my commercial seminars, and from there I started doing more of those and getting bookings for in-office consulting to the point that I had to train other consultants, real fast! Early in 1983, we hired a secretary and moved into a small office.

*Training centers* are another great opportunity that fits into multiple categories. Speakers can be invited as a guest lecturer or regular faculty, or you can even launch your own training center.

**DR. JOEL ROSENLICHT**

What really happened was that as I was traveling around and I saw the way presentations were being done, it allowed me to start thinking about the idea of starting my own teaching center. We launched this in the mid-80s and called it the Connecticut Dental Implant Institute. I built out a 600–700 sq. ft. teaching facility, so we put on our own educational activities on bone grafting and implants, and it has morphed into so many different things over the years as technology has changed.

At that time, there were a few other teaching centers, but not like it is today, and back then, there were not lecturers like there are today, for whom it is almost a career move. I did it as an adjunct to my practice and because I enjoyed it, and it kept me current and up to date, and it gave me an opportunity to be on the cutting edge of the profession. Implants were an important start for me, but over the years we have done a lot more than just implants—like bone grafting, cone beam technology, and now stem cells and bone morphogenic proteins. I've had an opportunity to really be able to use the newest technologies, and I think a lot of that came from my opportunity to be involved with industry as I was doing these programs.

We also established a ski symposium that went on for 27 years, and the only reason we stopped it within the last year or two was because the level of effort to put that on kept growing.

## Marketing Tips from Speakers

Everyone wants an instantaneous path to a successful speaking business. I don't think there is one, but I've learned a bit along the way. Most speakers do not have great success with cold calling (or cold emailing) meeting planners. This is an industry of relationships and reputations, so networking is key.

### TIP: ASK FOR REFERRALS FROM YOUR AUDIENCE YOU JUST WOWED.

**LINDA MILES**

In my consulting business, I never marketed much because I stayed so busy just by word of mouth. What's so ironic is that most of my clients didn't want anyone to know that they had hired a consultant because they didn't want to look like they didn't know what they were doing. As a result, they would never refer me to someone in their community, but they would sing my praises to people from out of town. They would say, "My wife and I will travel to wherever you are speaking to learn more from you, but do me a favor and never come speak here in my town because I don't want anyone else to know about you!" However, I would hand them three postcards about my speaking and consulting services and say to them, "I know you have classmates or colleagues who would benefit from the work we have done here together today; do me a favor and drop this in the mail to three people." And that worked!

Also, team members move around all the time, so I always asked them, "Do you know the names of any practices that could benefit from what you've learned today?" and they would say, "Oh man, do I!" So, they gave me a lot of referrals.

## TIP: TAKE EVERY OPPORTUNITY TO ESTABLISH YOURSELF AS AN EXPERT.

### DR. ROY SHELBURNE

What doesn't work for me is cold calls or blind emails... there has always been an advocate or connection, someone who has heard me, or heard of me, perhaps through some kind of organization that networks, and been asked, "Who have you had speak that has been good?"

I'll ask people who invite me to speak how they heard about me. It's all over the board. There was an interview I did with Chairside Magazine and that resonated with the public... scouts at various meetings have helped develop other engagements... and word of mouth and Google searches on my topic... I've tried to track some of this so I could focus on how to promote myself, and to be honest with you, I'm more effective when I don't.

People call and invite me, and then we start the period of negotiation. I am very honest and open to tell people when I am not an expert in the area they are looking for and quickly give them a referral for a better fit. Then, some time later, these same people will call me back and invite me to speak on the area that I am an expert in! The highest compliment I get is when someone I've spoken for invites me to come back.

Besides Linda Miles being instrumental in getting me started, Dr. Charles Blair (one of the most amazing men in dentistry, especially in the billing and coding area), called me the next spring (2011) and asked me if I had ever written before, and I said, "No." He was in negotiations to purchase the Insurance Solutions newsletter, and he was looking for contributing writers. So, I agreed to write an article, and I described what I had gone through. Any time you write, it opens up a large audience who can take a look at what you've produced and say, "Hey, we'd like this person to be able to share this information live with us." He eventually asked me to be a full-time contributing writer with his organization, which opened up another door. I was given an opportunity to study at the feet of one of the greats on a day-to-day basis and be exposed to the most up-to-date information and questions that offices were struggling with every day, which I then had to work through to be able to give them the appropriate information. This helped establish my position as an expert in the field.

Any time you have an opportunity to share your information, take it. Make sure that you present yourself in a way that is genuine and demonstrates concern with the education and the expertise, and make sure that you are the person to contact if someone needs this topic addressed.

**RACHEL WALL, RHD**

Enlist your host or a friend to pass out cards to scouts as they come in. You can also give them a CD/DVD of you presenting material or even a book or article on your topic.

## The Gifts of Having a Mentor

**Dr. Joel Rosenlicht**
I think a pivotal moment for my speaking career was being on the podium with people who I really had high, high respect for. Dr. Carl Misch was like a mentor to me early on because he was one of the first people who really impressed me as a speaker, as a young educator, and as a leader. It did have a lot of meaning to me, because I learned a lot in my early years, not necessarily from my specialty, but from the general dentists who were pioneers in the early stages of implant dentistry that I got to meet and be friends with.

After meeting some of these people, not only from this country but from all over the world, I really respect the ones who have the ability to speak and explain what they do—not only their successes but also their failures. I always try to give a balanced approach to the presentations because not everybody can do everything well all of the time. There is a certain amount of honesty that needs to be expressed whenever you are talking about someone's new technology in medicine or dentistry.

**Dr. Tom Kepic**

My break came when I was asked to campaign for the position of Director for the American Board of Periodontology ('06-13). Many consider it the highest academic position in my specialty of periodontics. A colleague, Dr. Claude Nabers, nominated me. I called Dr. Nabers and asked if he had really done that, and he said, "Yes, you will be a great Director"! I called another mentor, Dr. Jim Mellonig, and he also agreed and encouraged me. I won the election and it gave me a great deal of visibility and credibility. Collaborating with my peers on the Board offered another dimension of knowledge. It propelled me to a level I never dreamed possible. Believe in those younger than you, as they can also succeed.

**Dr. Tanya Brown**

I have been blessed with so many people who have touched my life over the years. One of the people who has made the most significant impact is Linda Miles. She has been an amazing mentor and friend, and she has helped me as well as so many others in countless ways. A few years ago, she invited me to speak with her at the Hinman 100 Year Anniversary Dental Event. That was a big-time presentation! They have also had Dr. Gordon Christensen and other big names on their programs; people who I feel are way out of my league. What an honor and privilege to be a part of such a prestigious organization. This helped catapult my speaking career.

# Sponsors

Sponsors are companies who want to attend a meeting in hopes of selling their services to the attendees. They want to display their goods (outside the meeting room) and also be recognized from the podium by the host and/or the speaker as a sponsor of the program.

Sponsors will only want to help support your honorarium if there is some correlation between their product/services and your lecture. You can invite a sponsor to attend one of your lectures or have them call a previous host to see whether you are a good fit for them. Be careful to only accept sponsorship support on behalf of products that you use and truly believe in. Nothing turns off an audience faster than a phony paid mouthpiece.

**Dr. Tim Silegy**
There are pluses to speaking on behalf of a company, but I think you have to sincerely believe in the product you are promoting. The audience will see right through you if you don't!

**Dr. Roy Shelburne**
I try to develop relationships with sponsors. Meetings are suffering, and they are trying to make the numbers work too. Sometimes their honorarium is not enough to meet your needs, so if you have a relationship with a sponsor who is willing to maybe defray some of those expenses,

then it can turn my "No" into a "Yes." But these sponsor relationships should be something that is congruent with your message.

**Dr. Tanya Brown**
When I am considering being sponsored by a particular company, first it must be a company that I believe in and have personally worked with. As a practicing dentist, it adds huge credibility when I can share that I personally use a particular product or service in my practice. Of course, sponsors want a return on their investment, and ultimately for the attendees to be able to use their product or service.

Note: Check with each sponsor to determine if there are any products or services that they really need to be mentioned in order to feel that they got their money's worth. Most sponsors do NOT expect you to be an infomercial; in fact, they would rather you weren't. What they really want is for you to incorporate their product/service into your lecture as a valued solution to your topic.

They may offer to supply you with some corporate slides, and if they do, I recommend you either personalize them to match your slides, or specifically call out to the audience, "These slides are courtesy of XYZ Company and are being included so that I don't mess up their product." None of this should require that any particular length of time be spent, only that which is natural to the flow of the talk.

PAR

# HOW TO BUILD A COMPELLING AND MEMORABLE PRESENTATION

# CHAPTER 5
## TOPIC SELECTION

### Start with Why

None of us sit down to write a mediocre talk, but lots of them are out there, so how do we ensure that we are the ones writing a STELLAR talk, one that makes an impact and drives real change?

It starts with understanding something about human nature. Our brains are hardwired to process different stimuli in different areas. We process features, benefits, facts, and figures in our neo-cortex. Unfortunately, this part of our brain doesn't drive behavior. That happens in the limbic center. That is where we experience feelings, which in turn control our behavior and our decisions. So, in a nutshell, we can feed our audiences all the data we want, but if we haven't touched their feelings, we haven't driven behavior.

In Simon Sinek's TED Talk on "Start With Why" (https://www.youtube.com/watch?v=IPYeCltXpxw), he explains that everyone knows what they do (the products or services they offer) and some people are clear on how they do it (their value proposition). However, very few people can

articulate why they do it. What is their higher purpose, their reason for getting going each morning? He calls this the Golden Circle.

Discovering our purpose can be a funny thing. I believe that our values drive our purpose, and if we have clarity on those two things, most things in our life become clearer. My values were formed as a child. My father taught me that if my integrity was intact, lots of other things naturally fell into place (honesty, work ethic, human kindness, etc.)  My mother taught me to look at the world with a sense of adventure. She showed me how to meet calamity with opportunity and to have childlike wonder at all that nature offered.

These values have led me to a place where I have an abundance of gratitude for all the blessings I have in my life. You see, up until about 12 years ago, I looked at life through the eyes of a bewildered victim, trying harder and harder to right the ship but never understanding why things just seemed to get worse. I thought my purpose was to be a good person, a good mother, and a good employee, but somehow, I just never seemed to be able to live up to my own impossibly high standards of what that was supposed to be. Then a series of dramatic events brought about some major changes for me, and in my humbled state, I was graced with some loving and wise mentors. Not a week has gone by since then that I haven't been filled with gratitude that my life just keeps getting better, and new mentors just keep showing up for me.

Thus, my why values (integrity, kindness, and childlike wonder) have given birth to a new purpose—to be of service to others in their lives, as so many have been for me.

**Spend the time to dig deep for clarity on your why, how and what.**

## Ask yourself WHY 3-5 times

Why is this topic important? Why has it impacted you and why will it impact others? Keep going until you find that emotional tug, that gotcha moment. Start your talk there.

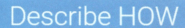

## Describe HOW

This new tool is different or game-changing for your audience.

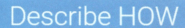

## Fill in the details

By providing the features, benefits, facts and figures as proof.

## No, You Are NOT the Hero

With this in mind, you sit down to write your talk. You know what you want to talk about. You are the expert, and you know what a difference your great idea will make for others, right? You are going to be their HERO!

NOT!

A true mentor understands that the audience is the hero, the ones responsible for saving their world from all sorts of bad outcomes or for reaching the top of some summit. You, the expert, are just a humble guide there to give them pointers and tools so that they will succeed in their quest.

It's like the story of Tenzing Norgay, the Sherpa who accompanied Sir Edmund Hillary on the first summiting of Mt. Everest. Over a period of nearly 20 years, Norgay had made

The Sherpa GUIDE Tenzing Norgay (left) and the HERO Sir Edmund Hillary (right)

Photo: George Band/Royal Geographical S

himself a part of every expedition that set out to put a man on the top of Mt. Everest. He had climbed as a lowly porter and as a respected member of the climbing team. He had accompanied large, confident armies on their way to the summit, but he had also gone to the mountain with a solitary climber. By 1953, he had probably spent more time on Mt. Everest than any other human being—and had come closer to its summit. And yet, when the day came, and he was the Sherpa guide that led Hillary on that momentous climb, it was Hillary who received the accolades, Hillary who was declared the hero.

That's right, you are NOT the hero! Not today anyway. You are the guide who has gone before and knows how to help others along on their journeys. Beware, though; heroes aren't really keen on being told what to do (remember your days as a hero). Rather, they feel a camaraderie from sitting around the campfire hearing stories of the guide's biggest challenges and how they were overcome. As the guide, your best approach is to share your own experiences—how you struggled, why you sought to try something different, the initial trial and error, and then finally, the success.

Also, think about how much information is appropriate. Inexperienced speakers often feel like they need to throw every bit of expertise they have into a lecture to prove to the audience that they are indeed worthy of their attention or in hopes that everyone will get something out of the lecture. The reality is that people hit overload when faced with too much to absorb and end up discarding everything. Don't forget, you will not be the only guide who this hero encounters! Since adults only tend to hang onto information that is useful to them at that particular moment, don't worry about being too narrow with your topic. If that is what drew someone to attend your lecture, that is exactly what they want from you!

Consider carefully which tools you will offer your hero. It should be less about what you want to talk about and more about what your audience needs to succeed.

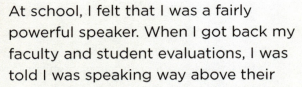

## DR. STEVEN SADOWSKY

At school, I felt that I was a fairly powerful speaker. When I got back my faculty and student evaluations, I was told I was speaking way above their heads. Now I have rearranged my slides to have a more progressive level of information and have more repetition to reinforce concepts. This year, I am going to reduce the number of slides and have more interactivity. I realized that I had made certain assumptions about what they already knew, and I didn't even realize I was making those assumptions.

One way to focus your topic is to identify the point of pain. However, be mindful that within a single group, different stakeholders have different needs. For instance:

If you are a specialist giving a talk on complications to your referrals, your audience's pain might be:

*How to reduce complications or find a new specialist to which to refer the patient.*

However, your pain might be:

*How to get more referrals? More patients? More profitable procedures? Reduce the complications of referral patients?*

Further, if you are doing this talk for another specialist and their referral network, that host's pain might be:

*Needs referrals to do things differently? Needs more referrals? Wants to look like a hero? Needs face time with referrals?*

Finally, if you have a sponsor, their pain might be:

*Needs clinician to appropriately address clinical relevance? Need's clinical differentiation in the hands of an expert?*

As you can see, it takes diligence to investigate all the needs and determine which direction you are going to take to solve these points of pain.

### DR. TIM SILEGY

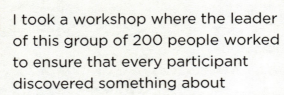

I took a workshop where the leader of this group of 200 people worked to ensure that every participant discovered something about themselves during the program. It was here that I was introduced to the idea of talking into people's listening. If people aren't ready to hear something that you are saying or if they don't believe your message is relevant to them, then you are not going to be very effective.

I once read a book about how to be an exceptional speaker. In it, the author suggests arriving to the venue early, in part to mingle with the audience and get to know them. I will frequently present myself incognito and ask people what they do or what they think about the topic. It generally gives me good insight into the minds of at least a few audience members. An added advantage is that I can now use these people during my talk to strengthen my credibility. "You know, I was talking to Ed before the program, and he said..." In an instant, the audience now wants to hear what I have to say because "Ed," one of their own, knows me. This brings me to an even more important topic, and perhaps the most important tool, that of how to generate the listening.

As I mentioned earlier, you could have a wealth of information, but if people aren't listening, you won't be effective. As I've become more experienced in lecturing, I've become progressively better at generating the listening of the audience. Simply stated, you must give the audience a REASON to listen to you. Human nature is such that people will only pay attention if they think that there is something in it for them. For example, my kickoff to almost all of my implant lectures is "Did you know..." or I will ask a question, such as "How would you all like to go back to your practice tomorrow and be able to increase your implant production by 30%?" These simple questions have instantly caused audience members to listen because they want to know "How can I do this?" In contrast, if I just went up there and started with "This is how I do my cases and they turned out really great..." then I'm just another person talking to them. Other questions might be "How many of you have ever had problem "X" when you are operating?" After a show of hands, I say, "Me too, and I've discovered a way to avoid that problem." When done effectively, this technique will keep your audience on the edge of its seat hanging on every word to get that pot of gold at the end of the rainbow.

On occasion, you may have to present to a group of people who don't really care about your topic, or harder still, may disagree with the premise of your discussion. In cases such as these, I start my lectures by discussing paradigms. I will typically do some type of participation exercise that illustrates a well-known paradigm and then go on to define a paradigm shift. By showing participants that preconceived ideas may prevent them from being open to something new, it will cause them to at least be willing to hear you out.

**DR. TANYA BROWN**

I've learned a lot by going back and listening to recordings of myself. What to say, how to say it differently... and that it's not about me, it's about them. It is challenging to appeal to a wide array of audience members. I have also learned that I want to help facilitate true learning, growth, and change and not just be a one-hit-wonder where I am in and out.

# Who Chooses What the Audience Will Remember?

When I come home from a conference, my husband always asks me, "What did you learn?" If I'm lucky, I can go through my memory of the schedule and pick out one key thing I learned from each talk. **As a speaker, do you know what you want this one key thing to be or are you leaving it up to chance?**

Nancy Duarte calls this notion of a key takeaway the big idea. She says in her book *Resonate* that a big idea needs to be:

- Your unique point of view on a topic;
- A clear statement of what's at stake for those who DO or DON'T adopt your point of view; and
- Written in the form of a sentence.

For instance, let's say you're giving a talk on social media and you title the lecture "The Importance of Social Media." What does that mean? Will you spend time going over social media's history, user statistics, all the various forms of social media, and so on? If so, what am I as an audience member supposed to get out of it?

Before you start to write your talk, spend time following Duarte's construct. Using the social media example, you realize that your unique view is that social media is more than just a photo gallery; it is a way to build and maintain relationships. You might assert that using social media correctly can either grow or shrink your network, so your ultimate big-idea statement might be Learn to Use Social Media to Build Relationships. Now when putting your talk together, you can easily see that history, statistics, and formats are irrelevant. Instead, you can tell stories. Maybe you open with a story about how before social media, you were trying to find a new CPA for your business. You had to call your friends and ask them one by one. Contrast that with today. Just last week you posted a request for a good desktop publishing software on Facebook. Lots of people responded, and one friend even introduced you to a graphic designer! The remainder of your talk should focus on best practices of how to build relationships using social media.

You see, audiences don't want more content, they want clarity! A confused mind always says, "No," so don't obfuscate the key point with extraneous details. You select what your KEY takeaway will be and ensure that the message comes through loud and clear.

A good rule of thumb is to ensure that you have a

# SUBJECT,

## AN ACTION,

### AND A RESULT
(of taking or not taking the action).

Two more examples:

Topic: **"Restorative Solutions"**

Putting ourselves in the role of the meeting planner, what do we think this lecture is about? Is this too vague?

What about

**"Restorative Solutions for the Edentulous Arch"?**

Okay, now we know a bit more, but are we inspired to hire this speaker?

Using Duarte's construct of a big idea, how about this?
**"Solutions for the Edentulous Patient That Restores Full Use of the New Replacement Teeth."**

Subject (edentulous patient), Action (solutions), Result (restores full use of the new replacement teeth)

Much better, right? Let's try another.

Topic: **"Practice Management"**

Well, we might think we know what this is about, but again, it is a catch-all topic.

What about

**"Growing Your Practice with Leadership Skills"?**

This certainly is more specific and more intriguing. Reading this, I would assume the program would only be for dentists and maybe office managers. And I would be wrong. Because here is the final version:

**"Become a Dental Team That Gets More of What You Want."**

Subject (dental team), Action (become), Result (more of what you want).

## Speaker Tips on Selecting a Topic

Speakers are inherently subject matter experts, but in today's information tsunami, it's tough to stand on the platform of being the expert of anything. Therefore, each speaker must decide how they want to go about selecting topics and building their reputation.

> ## TIP: FIND THE NUGGET WITHIN A TOPIC THAT THE AUDIENCE CAN BRING BACK TO THEIR PRACTICE. MAKE IT RELEVANT TO THE MAJORITY.
>
> **DR. JOEL ROSENLICHT**

That is honestly a real challenge. As far as selecting topics, I either choose my own, or someone asks me to speak on a particular topic. The harder part is getting all the information to make that topic pertinent. How do you prepare for that lecture? How do you want to present it? What is the content that is clear and concise? How are you going to be able to show it for those that are visual learners as well as those that need clear oral communication?

Different people in the audience are going to take away different things, so you have to try to hit that mean where you are going to be able to satisfy the majority of people's needs so that they feel as though they have gotten their money's worth or that they have learned something that they can bring back to their practice.

**TIP: PICK A TOPIC YOU ARE PASSIONATE ABOUT. IT WILL FUEL YOUR RESEARCH, YOUR HOURS OF WORK, AND YOUR ACTUAL DELIVERY.**

**DR. TOM KEPIC**

Many years ago, Dr. James Mellonig invited me to lecture at University of Texas San Antonio Health Science Center Department of Graduate Periodontics. When I asked him what topic he wanted me to speak on he said "anything you want to". While I struggled with how broad it was, I realized he wanted me to speak to my passion. My audience would find it interesting if I put in the effort. Lectures require time and effort to develop, but it won't seem like work if you follow your passion.

I've been passionate about the subject of Prognosis. As a Director for American Board of Periodontology, I recognized that most candidates were weak on establishing an accurate prognosis for a periodontally compromised tooth, as was I! So I went into research mode and learned as much as I could and now I routinely lecture about it.

I also lecture on other topics I am passionate about: Bone regeneration around teeth and Proper Periodontal Maintenance around teeth and dental implants.

Charles Handy the British social philosopher who helped form the London School of Business said, "In order to really learn a topic, you need to speak about it, because only when you speak about it can you fully grasp what it is that you should be learning."

## TIP: USE AUDIENCE EVALUATIONS TO DRIVE YOUR TOPIC DEVELOPMENT— THEY KNOW WHAT THEIR POINTS OF PAINS ARE!

**LINDA MILES**

I never created my own material. At the bottom of my evaluation form, I asked (1) What did you enjoy most about today's lecture? and (2) What would you like to hear at future programs? So my attendees really created the topics.

## TIP: START WITH YOUR AREA OF EXPERTISE AND LET LOOSE YOUR INNER STORYTELLER.

### DR. ROY SHELBURNE

When people ask me what I talk about, my answer is, "Nobody is ever more surprised to find out than I am!" It does change depending on the group I am with (I do my research to find out what their concerns are beforehand). I just try to speak from the heart and present in a way that I feel that they will benefit from, knowledge-wise, and from a core point of view. Once you get started, and you are telling the story, it kind of happens organically. I'm not one who is good about putting things on paper and scripting things, so I kind of share with my audience. I want them to walk away feeling a bit better about themselves and more focused about who they are and what they want to be. From that first presentation until now, that's what I do.

**DR. TIM SILEGY**

I'm a Steven Covey fan. In his Seven Habits of Highly Effective People, he lists one of those habits as being "begin with the end in mind." I start by determining what I want the audience to get out of my presentation. Then I think about how I can generate their listening. Next, I figure out how to best present the information. Will I use PowerPoint, a flip chart, white board, or a combination? Do I depend on graphics and pictures or bullet points and text? From there, I think about the cases I have that can be used to illustrate the points I want to make.

### DR. STEVEN SADOWSKY

My research is on treatment planning and implants, and I've published widely in this area. When I go out, people want to know about treatment planning (based upon a survey in Canada, it is the number-one thing people want to know with regard to implant dentistry), so it's well received. I bring cases from the clinic or others I've received and focus on pivotal decision-making and on how we can be more of a prognosticator. I've actually used the analogy of a crystal ball... that we are actually being asked to be psychics, we are being asked what is going to last 10–15 years. We have to do this based upon limited information, and even then, the information is flawed based upon a variety of clinical factors. So, I teach that the more data that we can bring to the table (not just institutional data, but even a particular practitioner's data), the more we can help people make better decisions. This ends up being something very near and dear to an attendee's heart.

**DR. TANYA BROWN**

My favorite topic is Case Acceptance with a Total Team Approach, because when every team member is setting the stage for patients to say "yes"; that's when real magic happens! When selecting a topic, I draw from my own past experience as a dental assistant, dental administrator, associate Dentist, and now as an owner dentist and speaker/consultant. I look at what I have learned in dentistry and what I wished someone would have taught me! I also take into consideration the feedback from my audiences and consulting clients and things that people are struggling with. So that is where I start, and then I try to build a framework around that. Remember, you don't have to be a "jack of all trades", you will be more successful if you speak on topics that you are passionate

If You Fail to Plan, You Plan to Fail

Topic selection and clarity are the MOST important factors in a successful lecture.

# CHAPTER 6
## THE CART BEFORE THE HORSE: RESEARCH YOUR TOPIC FIRST

### BRAINSTORMING

There are many methods for brainstorming out there, but everyone agrees that it is the time to include everything. Personally, I cut up scratch paper to simulate notecards (ever the recycler) and write down one idea per card. If the idea is too broad, I break it down to the details and crumple up the broad idea card. I go on tangents with my ideas and generate more cards. I go to webpages I have bookmarked and write down those ideas (I capture my sources on the back of these cards). At this stage, don't be stingy or edit.

| | |
|---|---|
| **Follow all leads and collect ideas.** | • Research peer-reviewed journals, articles, blogs, even social media. Look for what insights and knowledge will help support and clarify your idea. Collect evidence for your case and against your case.<br><br>• Ask a peer to contribute their thoughts. Ask someone outside the field to contribute their thoughts. |
| **Who is your audience and what does their daily life entail?** | • Detail what tools or skills are needed to implement your idea.<br><br>• What problem do they face that you have a solution for? If you were to stop there, what would the first objection be? If you can answer that, then what would be the objection to that answer? Keep cycling through this exercise to flesh it out. |
| **Research things (or people) that might be roadblocks to your idea.** | • Find out if there are alternate solutions. Know everything about the competition and what makes your idea unique.<br><br>• Determine what risks might exist for your audience if they take action.<br><br>• Know the costs (explicit and implicit) of adopting this new idea. |

| | |
|---|---|
| **What is the benefit to your idea?** | • How are things today and how will they be tomorrow?<br>• Are the benefits measurable (time, money, outcomes) or are they intangible (cohesive team, decreased safety risks, marketing). |
| **What are the risks/ hardships of adopting your idea?** | • Is time or money going to be required to get started?<br>• How can the risk of failure be minimized?<br>• Who might be resistant and how can they be brought on board? |

And then I play the two-year-old child and keep asking, "Why?" Every assumption must stand up to at least three whys. Every answer becomes a unique notecard. I don't worry about reading them or editing them, I just keep writing.

For me, this process takes multiple sittings because what happens is as I dump my ideas onto paper, new ideas get a chance to rise up. My husband laughs because I will have little scraps of paper everywhere! Eventually, however, there comes a moment when I think I've exhausted all avenues, and it's time to take stock of where I am.

NOTE: Another of my favorite brainstorming methods is "The Six Thinking Hats" (http://sixthinkinghats.com). This model has you look at a topic from a variety of viewpoints such as factual, emotional, challenges, benefits, feelings, and actions.

## TIP: ACCESS WHATEVER RESOURCES YOU CAN SO YOU DON'T HAVE TO RE-CREATE THE WHEEL, THEN LAYER YOUR OWN UNIQUE POINT OF VIEW ON TOP OF THAT.

### DR. STEVEN SADOWSKY

It seems that there are different cogs that turn at different rates. Doing the research for a new talk is really rough. It feels very slow and laborious. As the body of the work forms some continuity, it gets more exciting and speeds up, and then there is a moment when I actually get an adrenaline rush because I can see the entire thing coming together. This whole process of putting a presentation together is not linear. I'm not sure how I could speed up the parts that are slow.

One of the things that has really helped was when Dr. Charlie Goodacre (Loma Linda University) gave me a number of his presentations as a starting place. He was a pioneer in terms of releasing material from the so-called intellectual property stigma. Many people think if you let someone else use your material, you will no longer be the messiah. But he believed, as do I, that it's not the material, it's the person delivering it that matters. Ultimately, making these materials public benefits everyone and advances the educational forum.

So, taking a page from his book, as the President of the American Prosthodontic Society (starting in February 2016), I want to develop an electronic library so that all of the members can share our collective amassed material with each other. If you have a vision for something that should happen during your tenure, that is a great opportunity.

## SORTING

At this point, I create a massive game of solitaire on my dining room table with my notecards. I start by stacking them into logical groups. I will start with one definition of what makes a group, and then quickly learn that these groups need to be broken down into smaller groups with entirely different criteria. There is no right or wrong here except you must never force a notecard into a group it doesn't really belong with. As such, I often end up with a few stray notecards that don't fit anywhere.

It never ceases to amaze me how often my own talks morph during this process. Things I thought were key points turn out not to fit into these logical piles. (I still save these spurious key points, but for another lecture or another article.) Other things I hadn't considered suddenly rise to the top, often requiring another round of research!

Once I think that I have completed the sorting process, I write a title notecard for the top of each stack. The title for each pile should be in the form of a complete sentence.

### DR. STEVEN SADOWSKY

When I was in grad school, we did a lot of evidence-based research, very academic, but I figured out that that did not have a lot of currency with attendees. I would put in too much theoretical information, which created a very long diving board for a very small splash.

I could feel the energy in the room—the lack of attentiveness... what they wanted was the bottom line, not the nitty-gritty. I learned I had to re-create this approach for more of a recreational result. It took me awhile to learn how to balance the research with how to do this in a practical way. I had to be able to deliver the takeaway from these academic points, the why does this matter nuggets, because it turns out that there are some counter-intuitive conclusions that make it very interesting. People end up being appreciative of this in the clinical environment.

## CHUNKING

Have you ever played that sliding puzzle where there are tiles in a slotted square box that you have to move around until you solve the puzzle? Chunking is a bit like that.

Chunks can be determined by a myriad of criteria: chronological, topical, pros/cons, before/after, cause/effect, proof of concept, and so forth. As with the sorting process, there is no right or wrong way to chunk except you must never force a group of notecards into a chunk that it doesn't really belong with.

As I start to move my stacks of notecards around, I slide entire sections from here to under there, or out from this chunk into a new chunk. I think about my audience and what they may or may not already know, and I think about what order makes the most sense in order to approach this information. At last, I have all my stacks organized in some fashion, but it has become clear that not everything really fits into my chunks.

Now comes the moment of truth.

## EDITING
## (and benching some of your darlings)

So far everything we have done has been without limits, without boundaries, and without judgment, but now we have to face the fact that there are some stray notecards and some stray stacks. These strays just don't belong in this talk! In fact, we may discover that we have brainstormed our way into more than one talk!

I believe in selecting ONE key message to deliver to your audience. People can't absorb everything you know, so give them clarity on one thing. The chunking process helps reveal what our key message is (and it's sometimes different than what we started with!). Once you have this defined, your talk should include no more than two to four sub-points that tie directly to your one key message. Those other points? Bench them! Save them in a file for the next talk you have to write.

Now it's time for the next set of cuts. Go through each stack and test each point against your one key message. Is it necessary, is it helpful, and is it useful? If it doesn't fit, bench it. If it's nice to have but not need to have, put it to the side for now.

At last, you have the outline for your lecture, a lecture that matters!

## DR. JOEL ROSENLICHT

The audience today is pretty bright, and I've always been concerned (knowing that there are always going to be people in the audience who are smarter than I am) that I might say something that is incorrect, so I do think you have to do good preparation.

I always call the contact point in advance, a couple of times. The first time, they tell me what they want me to lecture on, how much time I will have, and what the audience is going to look like. Then, when I get an idea in my mind about what I want to present, I call them back to find out if I am on the right track, and then right beforehand, I call them back again to review what I have developed to ensure that this is what they were thinking about when they asked me to speak. This works most of the time for most of the audience, and I have a pretty good idea what the person who invited me to speak is looking for and can hit that mark fairly well.

## DR. TOM KEPIC

I lecture on two topics; periodontics and leadership/management. I am also the editor for the Gum Line Newsletter for wsperio.org.

Peter Drucker (the "father" of modern management) was a patient in my periodontal office. He was on a two-month maintenance schedule and I personally cleaned his teeth. I scheduled one hour for his visit, and once I finished the procedure (typically 20 mins), I asked him a whole host of questions. He was commanding very high consulting fees and I was getting his expertise for no charge. He knew how passionate I was about business, so he nourished my quest for knowledge. His wisdom became the bedrock of my management lectures.

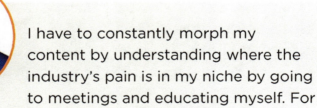

## DR. ROY SHELBURNE

I have to constantly morph my content by understanding where the industry's pain is in my niche by going to meetings and educating myself. For instance, I'm a member of the AACD (made up of dentists who work for insurance companies as well as the insurance agencies who actually deal with claims every day) to get behind the curtain to hear what they are concerned about and where they think fraud and abuse is happening. Knowing that information, I'm equipped with what I need to be able to share with my audiences.

## DR. STEVEN SADOWSKY

As far as original presentations, I've spent hundreds of hours putting my presentations together. I am currently putting a new presentation together on implants versus natural teeth, and I've already put in over 40 hours. I review existing presentations (my own, ones from friends, etc.) to see how much I can repurpose, and then I do an outline on what I want to demonstrate (what is my angle?). Evidence can lie if you don't know how to interpret it, so I have to dive deep to get where I can find an algorithm or branching tree to hopefully help people to achieve more predictable results. Then, each bit of research brings about support or new branches. It's like a treasure hunt. Finally, once the information is all collected and refined, there is a creation of the bridges from point to point. This is a very important part of the task, and all this takes the most of my time.

To develop a new aspect to an existing lecture, I will bring in new cases that we have done and then incorporate new research I have found or that has changed in recent years. The basics are still the same, but I might add in ~10 slides.

## RACHEL WALL, RHD

I'm at the point now where I'm not creating many new lectures from scratch anymore, but when I do, I always start with an outline on paper first. I like to try to chunk it down into three sections. Next, I pull content from past lectures and repurpose as much as I can. I will go through past articles or ezines (and Evernote, where I collect ideas) to pull relevant things out. I also get a lot of ideas from business books I read that apply to dental topics.

# CHAPTER 7
## NEVER JUST WRITE A POWERPOINT

As you look at everything you've selected to go into your talk, be brutal with yourself. Just because you know everything that there is to know on your subject (in this moment) doesn't mean that the audience wants to know all of that! What the audience wants is CLARITY. They want just enough information to make a yes or no decision and to know how to get started.

I look at outlines like building a house. You want a foundation, walls, and a roof.

**WHY** should I care? The foundation should be about the present state of things in order to establish the groundwork for where we are today.

**HOW** will this make my life better? The walls are the supporting structure, the bones of the building, to establish the reasons why we are proposing this new idea, including the results that come from this idea or the consequences of rejecting this idea.

**WHAT** action do I need to take? The roof is the top of the building; it is what most protects a structure from harm and decay; similarly, actions taken to implement this new idea will protect and shield the idea and allow it to prosper.

In each of these subsections, you should try to include three elements: a story, proof, and contrast between what is and what could be.

# three-act story structure

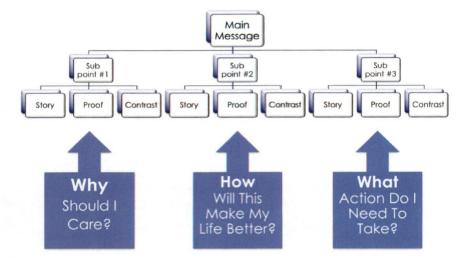

Using our restorative lecture example, you might have an outline something like this:

**"Solutions for the Edentulous Patient That Restores Full Use of the New Replacement Teeth"**

i. Patient's current lifestyle challenges.
   a. Story of a patient who used to compete in BBQ competitions and now can't even eat his world-famous ribs (video of him and his wife as he talks about his sadness).
   b. Facts about current and projected edentulism in US.
   c. What treatments (or lack of treatments) existed in the past and how patients suffered (with poor fitting dentures).

ii. Various current solutions with pros and cons.
   a. Solution A: Story of a patient, case photos, and data on solution.
   b. Solution B: Story of another patient, case photos, and data on solution.
   c. Solution C: Story of another patient, case photos, and data on solution.

iii. How to do YOUR solution (Solution D).
   a. Step-by-step case photos of your original patient.
   b. Data on solution.
   c. Video of patient testimonial and the two of you enjoying his ribs at a cookout.

By keeping a single patient as the overarching storyline, you are able to keep people in suspense to find out if he will be happy again and tie your solution to his happiness. People will always act on *why* before they act on data.

Let's try this for our Practice Management talk.

**"Become a Dental Team That Gets More of What You Want"**

i.  Typical top-down leadership model.
    a.  What top-down leadership model means and how it looks in a dental practice.
    b.  Facts about current turnover or satisfaction levels in dental practices.
    c.  Story of a client who had high turnover due to disharmony in the practice.

ii.  Optional leadership models tried over the years.
    a.  Solution A: Explanation of model, data on success and story of a practice using this (or quote from an employee in this system).
    b.  Solution B: same.
    c.  Solution C: same.

iii. How to do YOUR solution.
    a.  Detailed explanation on how to implement the model, roles and responsibilities, and pitfalls to avoid.
    b.  Testimonials from other practices that have adopted this new model.
    c.  Final contrast of how things are today versus how they could be if this is adopted with a call to action.

## DR. JOEL ROSENLICHT

I think you have to lay out an outline in advance of what you are going to talk about. Focus on what aspects of that topic you know a lot about. If you don't know a lot about the topic, there is no reason you can't ask the audience for their input. I think that this kind of dialogue with the audience is important.

I try to get an outline and try to frame it to follow some kind of pattern—start with a beginning, then move into why or how I do something, and hopefully show an end result that gives me the chance to show why I did something one way over another, given that there are many, many ways of doing it.

## RACHEL WALL, RHD

As I am putting the flow together, I use a mix of content and activities and review to the best of my ability. I always try to do a review before a break now (I even have a note on my computer that reminds me to do this!).

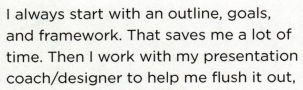

## DR. TANYA BROWN

I always start with an outline, goals, and framework. That saves me a lot of time. Then I work with my presentation coach/designer to help me flush it out, and then I start the process of tweaking, revising, practice, practice, practice, revise some more, practice more, and if it feels good, I go live with it. Then, based upon feedback from the audience, I might revise some more and keep going, or I might ditch it all together. I can't become attached to these talks because if it's not impactful, I have to get rid of it.

# CHAPTER 8
## IT STARTS WITH PARTS

### Why Use Slides at All?

First, let's get this often-asked question out of the way.

**Q: I was told I shouldn't use slides at all. Why do you recommend them?**

A: At least 65 percent of the adult population are visual learners.[1] What that means is that their memory is tied to what they have seen, so if you don't show them anything, they won't remember anything.

I believe that slides should only be used for two reasons. The primary reason is to give the audience visuals to enhance learning and retention (memory moments). Second, it can help the speaker stay on point with visual cues.

The other thing I hear all the time is...

**Q: How many slides should I have for a one-hour talk?**

A: Slides are free, so you should have no more and no less than you need to convey your message with clarity and emotion. Anyone who gives you a rule of thumb is making things up.

---

1.   http://info.shiftelearning.com/blog/bid/350326/Studies-Confirm-the-Power-of-Visuals-in-eLearning

The simplest starting point is to ensure that each slide contains only one idea. You can start with typing each notecard as a slide, ensuring that the title is a declarative sentence. Strip out all the ancillary information and put that into your notes or into a handout. Slides should NOT contain everything you are going to say.

If you look at popular slide decks on places like SlideShare, you will see that today's trend is to have the following:

- Less text, larger fonts.
- More images, bigger images.
- Infographics instead of charts or data.

**LINDA MILES**

My previous approach to designing slides was to put as few words as possible in large font on each slide. Once I saw the word or phrase, I was off and running with my stories, but I know it was a very boring thing to look at.

However, it's also why I am so excited to be working with Margy now because she gave my bland slides the pictorial stories, and the ones who are visual learners LOVE my slides now! I can't wait to go out there because I feel like I have a whole new wardrobe.

### DR. TOM KEPIC

The myth is that somehow miraculously you can put together an excellent presentation just by opening Power Point. If one is to excel, I mean really excel, you must have a true professional that you can closely communicate with.

I have recently started working with Margy Schaller, my presentation designer—something I never knew existed. I thought I just had to go online and figure out this stuff for myself. I knew some people had slides that just looked amazing, and I didn't know how to do this. I will never do this on my own again.

### DR. TIM SILEGY

When I first started lecturing, I was constantly worried about having the correct number of slides. As I have matured as a speaker, I tend to focus more on getting the message across. Showing four cases of the same surgery doesn't give you more credibility.

PowerPoint and Keynote—they are just tools, and do we ALWAYS need them? What is more important is the right tool for the message and the group. Maybe it's a flip chart or a visual aid. I think there is too much of people writing out everything they want to say on a slide. Don't overuse slides! Keep more of it within the story. I think it should be reduced to only that which you HAVE to show.

Slide design is made up of the choices we make for fonts, colors, and images. Each of these has its own psychology, and how we choose to deploy these elements can actually affect our success.

# Font

You've worked on your presentation for months, carefully crafting the content, practicing the timing, and putting some slides together. You know your idea is well researched and will be a game-changer for your audience and you can't wait for their reaction!

Now it's the morning of the speech, and you need to pick out what you will wear. Do you show up in your most comfortable jeans and a souvenir T-shirt from your last vacation? Or should you spend time putting together a funny costume? Or is a tuxedo the best way to deliver your speech?

It's obvious to us that the clothes we wear tell our audience who we are on that day and provide a strong first impression. Fonts do the same thing for your presentation. The fonts we choose have subconscious associations based upon historical usage.
Let's take the example of the word Business:

| Serif | Sans Serif | Modern | Script | Hand-Drawn |
|---|---|---|---|---|
| Business | Business | BUSINESS | *Business* | Business |
| Times New Roman | Helvetica | moon | Zapfino | A Safe Place to Fall |
| Traditional, Trustworthy | Objective, Clean-Cut | Forward Thinking | Elegant, Unique | Friendly, Casual |

We can also be very intentional with fonts and use them to transform the emotional meaning of a word or a phrase:

**FUTURE PLANS**      **FUTURE PLANS**                *Future Plans*

This is great news because as a speaker, you now have one more tool in your toolbox to communicate who you are and what you stand for.

*Redesigned with a casual font for quotes*

USED WITH PERMISSION BY DR. GLENN KIDDER

However, there are several important warnings:

**WARNING #1:** If you choose the standard PowerPoint template, the default font is Calibri. While it is a clean Sans Serif font, our brain sees that and says, "Oh, I've seen that hundreds of times before; I don't need to pay close attention."

**TIP: AT THE VERY LEAST, GO TO THE DESIGN TAB AND CHOSE ONE OF THE OTHER STANDARD POWERPOINT (OR KEYNOTE) FONT COMBOS.**

**WARNING #2:** Don't go crazy with too many fonts on every slide. This comes across like a middle school project and decreases your credibility.

**TIP: CHOOSE A MAXIMUM OF TWO FONTS FOR YOUR PRESENTATION, THEN USE BOLD, ITALICS, AND FONT SIZE FOR VARIETY. ALTERNATIVELY, YOU CAN USE A UNIQUE FONT ON A PARTICULAR WORD OR PHRASE JUDICIOUSLY FOR MAXIMUM IMPACT (PERHAPS AS A RALLYING CRY FOR THE KEY TAKEAWAY).**

USED WITH PERMISSION BY PETER BARRY

**WARNING #3:** Font spacing is different from a Mac to a PC.

**TIP: DOUBLE-CHECK YOUR SLIDES IF YOU ARE SWITCHING PLATFORMS TO ENSURE THAT THERE ARE NO WEIRD WORD-WRAPS.**

**WARNING #4:** If you are not going to be using your own computer, your specialized fonts might not display as expected.

**TIP: IF YOU HAVE TO USE A SHOW COMPUTER, ASK IF YOU CAN PROVIDE THE FONT FILE TO THEM, AND THEN TAKE THE TIME TO GO THROUGH EACH OF YOUR SLIDES TO SEE HOW THEY LOOK. AS AN EXTRA PRECAUTION, YOU MIGHT WANT TO HAVE A BACKUP SLIDE DECK WITH STANDARD FONTS IN CASE THEY WON'T UPLOAD YOUR SPECIALTY FONTS.**

Another alternative is to convert your slide deck into a PDF where all the slides will show the same no matter what; however, you lose the ability to include any animation.

There are lots of sites where you can find free fonts. Some of my favorites are www.fontsquirrel.com and www.fontspace.com.

## Color

We all know that first impressions are less about what we say and more about how we appear. So too it is with our slides. We set the emotional tone right off the bat with the colors we choose.

*Colored font makes "FUN" stand out*

USED WITH PERMISSION BY DR FRANK GRAZIANO

*Colored font and background ties to the emotion of the slide*

USED WITH PERMISSION BY DR SONDA MOLDOVAN

All you have to do is start watching commercials or noticing advertisements and you will start to see how companies use color to influence our moods. One thing to note is that this chart is US-centric. If you are going to be speaking abroad, everything changes.

Do you recognize this?
It's the standard PPT color pallete, and while there are many more available in PPT, it can become... well... trite to use it. The same is true about using primary colors. They are just too basic. If you must use primary colors, try to use a richer version of the reds, blues and yellows.

I recommend designing your own color pallete! One of the best places that I find new color palletes is from packaging websites (just Google "packaging colors").

These folks have done market research as to what looks good together and what will be eye-catching and fresh.

Another good place to find color palettes is www.colorlovers. com . You can sort these by most loved to find out to which colors people currently respond.

*Use color to liven up your slides*

USED WITH PERMISSION BY DR TANYA BROWN

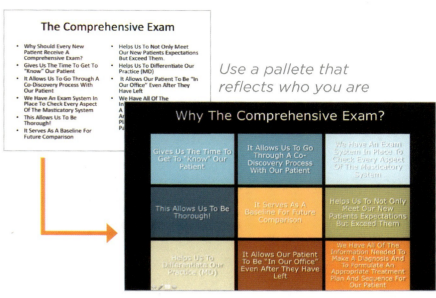

*Use a pallete that reflects who you are*

USED WITH PERMISSION BY DR FRANK GRAZIANO

I also encourage people to use their branding and their websites as a launching point. This can help you be more memorable as you reinforce your own brand. I've even gone so far as to use color as a psychological tactic. I went through all the websites of some important prospects I knew would be in my audience and took a snapshot of each one. Using a site called Color Scheme Designer, I was able to create a four-color pallete that tied them all together. It's like the mirroring body language we learn in Sales 101, but even more tricky because no one talks about this tactic!

## Images

**Wouldn't you love to increase recall of your presentation from 10% to up to** **70%?**

Recently, while I was checking into a hotel, the clerk told me how to get to the elevator. I turned around and realized I had not remembered anything she said past "go down the hall." When she saw my confusion, she pulled out a map and drew a line from where we were to the elevators. Boom, I had it! As previously mentioned, the majority of the population (including me) are visual learners, and we need to see something to remember it.

Graphic communication does what talking or text alone cannot do. Graphics expedite and increase our level of communication. They increase comprehension, recollection, and retention. Moreover, if you use pictures, you can touch people's emotions and attitudes as well as influence decision-making. Remember, people won't necessarily remember what you said, but they WILL remember how you made them feel.

One objection I've heard from speakers is that images are just eye candy but don't necessarily add anything of value. It actually depends on the type of visual selected. There are four different categories of visuals we can use in our presentations; decorative, representational, organizational and explanative.

## DECORATIVE

These are things like pictures of our families, our offices, our pets, and cartoons. They have no instructional potential, but can help humanize a presenter.

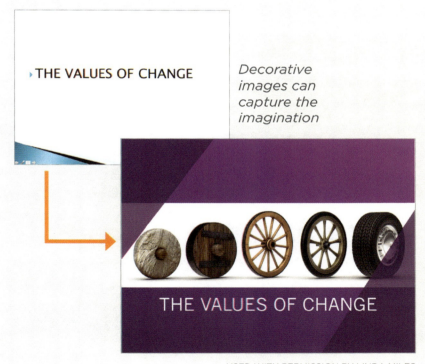

THE VALUES OF CHANGE

*Decorative images can capture the imagination*

THE VALUES OF CHANGE

USED WITH PERMISSION BY LINDA MILES

## REPRESENTATIONAL

These are symbolic images such as a yield sign instead of the word caution or an image of a clock instead of using the word time. These images have very little learning value but help declutter slides and draw attention to a particular concept.

*Representational images include icons*

USED WITH PERMISSION BY VIRGINIA MOORE

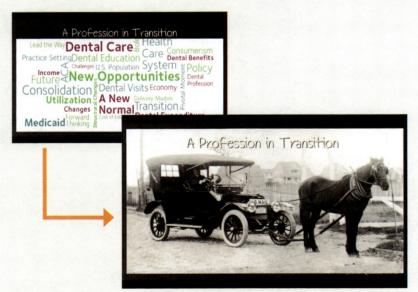

USED WITH PERMISSION BY DR. JOEL ROSENLICHT

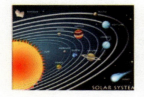

# ORGANIZATIONAL

These visuals help us understand how things fit together. For instance, instead of trying to verbally explain the solar system, an image gives the audience an immediate understanding of the concept. Charts and diagrams are included in this category. These visuals have an extremely high level of knowledge transfer and are invaluable to the visual learner.

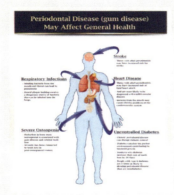

*Organizational images help an audience "see" what you are saying more clearly*

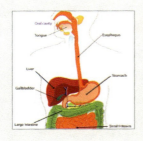

# EXPLANATIVE

This includes images or diagrams for systems or processes where your audience can see the entire flow and then break down the parts. For example, a lecture on the digestive system would be much more successful if the audience could see the entire system, then drill down to each part as the lecture progressed.

*Explanative images show how something works*

Fortunately, there are lots of places you can find free images and icons. Here are a few of my favorites:

- www.morguefile.com.
- www.iconmonstr.com.
- www.freeimages.com.
- www.compfight.com.

All these sites will tell you whether something requires credit to the source or not, and if it does, just put it in 8-point font down in the corner.

### RACHEL WALL, RHD

I just redid all my slides this year, and I went to a lot more images and a lot less text. I use a paid subscription service for my images, so I have good quality images. I like full background images rather than framed images. I try to use images that trigger me to the next point of content.

Clinical images are essential for a dental speaker. These images must be taken chairside in enough detail so that the audience can follow the procedure step by step. Don't ever assume your audience knows how to do something. Better to show it all than to lead someone astray or frustrate them by skipping a step.

## DR. JOEL ROSENLICHT

When I first started speaking, I wasn't a great speaker, and I didn't do a great job with my slides, but I think my message was good, and my success was due to being able to communicate well with the audience. I was on an international series of lectures (in the early '90s) and being sponsored by a major implant company to do five lectures over a two-week period of time (US, Europe, and South America). I remember clearly that when I got to Brazil to give this implant lecture at an Esthetic Dental Meeting, the chairman of that program came to my room the night before I was to present. He had heard me speak in Florida the week before. He thought my content was very good, but my slides/presentation were not up to the quality of this meeting. He asked to look at my slides, and he immediately told me which ones I could show and which ones I couldn't show, and it really devastated the presentation that I wanted to give. The sponsor was really upset that this had transpired, saying I had been all over the world and that this was an embarrassment to me... I got up the next morning to watch the other presentations (I was the only surgical presenter), and the quality of the esthetic presentations I was able to see was impeccable. I really got to see exactly what this guy was talking about. That was the beginning of my changing my presentations so that I could give them at a level that I was proud to present. So actually, for about six months, I didn't speak and focused on getting my images (and slides) so they were presentable at an improved level. My images at the time were rough... blood on them, not well framed, not cropped properly, not pristine... and the slides were boring to look at. Today's audiences expect more than just good content; in a way, they are expecting to be entertained. They want to be taught material that is easy to learn and easy to remember, and in order to do that effectively, there has to be some kind of a flamboyance or energy with your presentations. That's what I learned from that lecture. Even though I thought I was pretty good, you can always get better, and as a clinician, I didn't truly understand the value of presentation as a speaker.

## Layout

I believe layout is the chief culprit for the phrase "Death by PowerPoint," which describes the endless identical slides of text, bullet points, and a plain background. However, overdesign can be equally offensive. Whether you are combatting too much text or too much design, stick with the axiom "Less is More." The use of simplicity in today's noisy world can actually help us stand out, but it takes courage to strip everything away because it puts more burden on you the speaker to really know your stuff!

One of the reasons why we get so fatigued from slides is the canned templates. Everything looks the same as everything else, so why not design your own? I almost exclusively use the blank slide template and design from there. Below is not a template per se, but rather some ideas on how to arrange slides in a different way for visual interest.

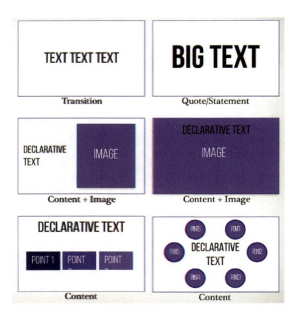

*Instead of listing things in bullets, lay them out in categories and use images instead of words*

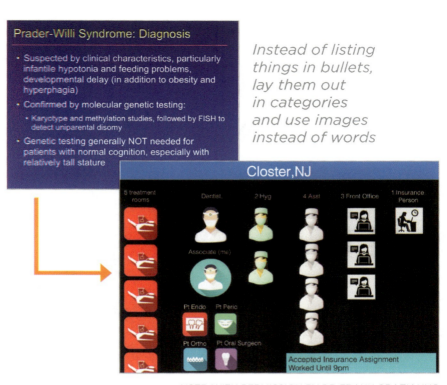

USED WITH PERMISSION BY DR FRANK GRAZIANNO

*Or use "Smart Art" to show a process*

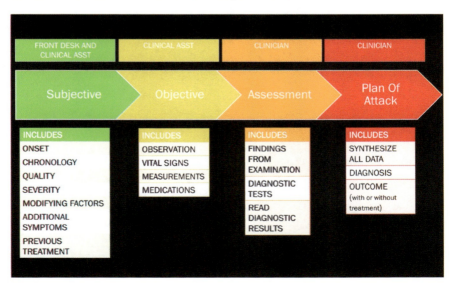

USED WITH PERMISSION BY CHRISTINE TAXIN

*Layout can be used to drive comprehension
by grouping things together.*

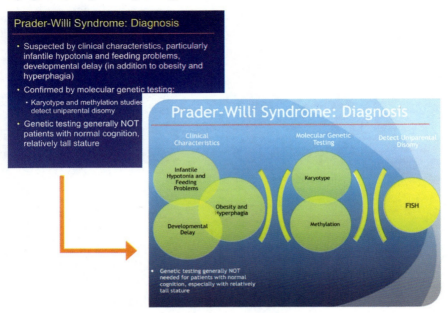

USED WITH PERMISSION BY DR ALISON HOPPIN

## The Rule of Thirds

Artists, photographers, and designers will tell you about the rule of thirds. In layman's terms, just draw a tic-tac-toe board on your slide (I set up my guide lines this way before I start designing). The intersecting points are the places our eye is naturally drawn. When you put an image of a person on a slide, have their eyes land on one of those intersections, or if you have a horizon or a doorway, have those natural lines align with one of your horizontal or vertical lines. You will find your images suddenly look more compelling!

## Displaying Data

Now we get to one of my favorite design elements—data. In today's world, we have to show data. Tell me the truth, aren't you convinced before you even show a data-heavy slide that the audience may not truly absorb the numbers and our goal is just proving that something is so? That is a universal truth, and it's why USA Today and other newspapers have started using data stories and infographics for everything!

I like to use things like proportional font size or graphics to demonstrate the differences between a large number and a small number, or instead of a chart, I use a row of icons matching the numbers I am portraying.

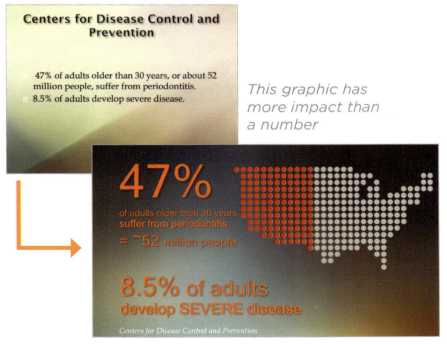

USED WITH PERMISSION BY DR. TOM KEPIC

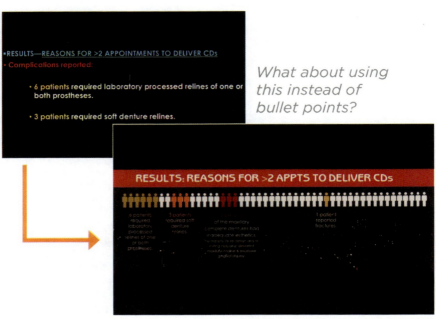

*What about using this instead of bullet points?*

USED WITH PERMISSION BY DR. ED McGLUMPHY

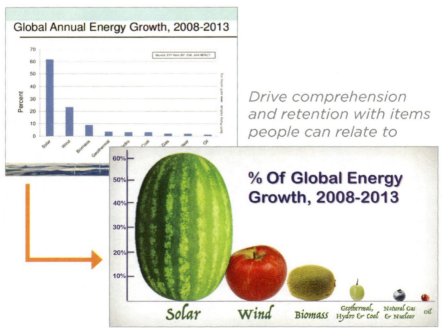

*Drive comprehension and retention with items people can relate to*

USED WITH PERMISSION BY DR. ED McGLUMPHY

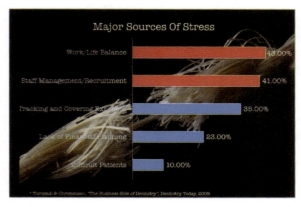

*Or add a photo to enhance the message*

Font, color, images, and layout are essential building blocks for your slides. They tell the audience who we are, or set a mood, or reinforce our brand. However, to create a truly compelling and memorable lecture, we need to understand how we learn and why we remember some things and forget others.

# CHAPTER 9
## WE ARE JUST WIRED THAT WAY!

In Chapter 6, we talked about how an emotional connection carries information longer. Our brains are hardwired to process different stimuli in different areas.

## Short- and Long-Term Memory

Researchers have been studying the effect of PowerPoints on lectures and whether it adds any value except entertainment. Though we certainly want to entertain our audiences, our ultimate goal is to provide information or training to our audience that will (a) result in a change in behavior or beliefs and (b) stick with our audience for as long as possible.

These research studies conclude that the traditional slide layout (title and bullets) has been shown to be less effective than using no slides at all. The problem is that people tend to read the slide and tune out, missing the information you are providing. However, if you use the ASSERTION-EVIDENCE (A-E) structure, recall has been shown to be **more accurate and longer lasting** than using no slides or the traditional slide layout.[1,2] The A-E structure is where a sentence headline states the main message of the slide. That message is then supported not by a bulleted list but by visual evidence: photos, drawings, diagrams, graphs, films, or equations.

1. Yue et al. (2013).
2. Aippersbach, S., Alley, M., and Garner, J. (2013). "Effect of Slide Design on How Much a Student Presenter Learns." Presented at the 2013 American Society for Engineering Education Annual Conference, Atlanta, GA, June.

*Redesigned with A-E Structure: headline and visual evidence*

USED WITH PERMISSION BY SANDY BAIRD

*Which one will have better comprehension and retention?*

USED WITH PERMISSION BY DR TOM KEPIC

Imagine your brain as an assembly line, with each area specializing in a certain task. As it turns out, long-term memories are built when a piece of information goes through multiple areas. In contrast, if the audience is only listening and reading, then the only part of the brain that is engaged is the temporal lobe. That is the area of our brain responsible for processing incoming sounds and visuals into meaningful information. By adulthood, we are exceptional at retaining short-term memories of things we learned this way.

But how do we create long-term memories? Long-term memories are built and maintained by more stable and permanent changes in neural connections widely spread throughout the brain. In other words, we have to stimulate multiple lobes simultaneously to create neural networks and synapses that will endure the decay of time. Thus, by using a clear statement (assertion) on the slide, our brain knows what to listen for. The visuals (evidence) further reinforce the message that our brain should be storing.

Storytelling also aids in developing long-term memories. You can tell the audience that you start out your weekend with some quiet reflection... or, you can bring them along on your journey. Ask them to close their eyes and, just for a moment, imagine the smell (frontal lobe) of bacon wafting into your room on a Saturday morning as you gently wake up. See (occipital lobe) the sun beaming into your bedroom and feel (parietal lobe) the nice stretch as you come into consciousness. As you are getting up, you hear (temporal lobe) the chirp of the birds greeting each other. This moment will stay with the audience; our brains are just wired that way.

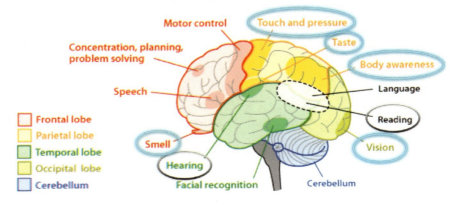

# Stimulate Senses To Increase Recall

- Motor control
- Touch and pressure
- Concentration, planning, problem solving
- Taste
- Body awareness
- Speech
- Language
- Reading
- Smell
- Vision
- Hearing
- Facial recognition
- Cerebellum

- Frontal lobe
- Parietal lobe
- Temporal lobe
- Occipital lobe
- Cerebellum

Here are some examples of how to incorporate sensory visuals:

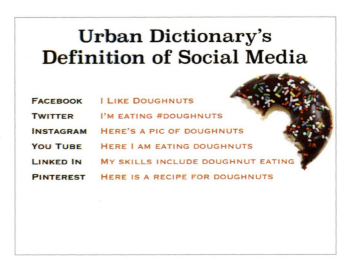

## Urban Dictionary's Definition of Social Media

| | |
|---|---|
| FACEBOOK | I LIKE DOUGHNUTS |
| TWITTER | I'M EATING #DOUGHNUTS |
| INSTAGRAM | HERE'S A PIC OF DOUGHNUTS |
| YOU TUBE | HERE I AM EATING DOUGHNUTS |
| LINKED IN | MY SKILLS INCLUDE DOUGHNUT EATING |
| PINTEREST | HERE IS A RECIPE FOR DOUGHNUTS |

USED WITH PERMISSION BY TONYA LANTHIER, RDH

Back Up Your Data

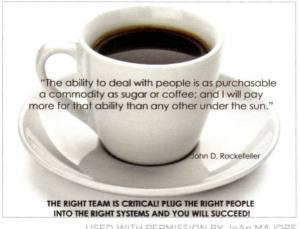

"The ability to deal with people is as purchasable a commodity as sugar or coffee; and I will pay more for that ability than any other under the sun."

John D. Rockefeller

**THE RIGHT TEAM IS CRITICAL! PLUG THE RIGHT PEOPLE INTO THE RIGHT SYSTEMS AND YOU WILL SUCCEED!**

USED WITH PERMISSION BY JoAn MAJORS

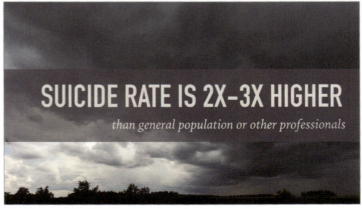

USED WITH PERMISSION BY DR SONDA MOLDOVAN

**DR. ROY SHELBURNE**

I don't use slides with huge bullets of information. I also try, periodically, to keep people engaged by throwing in an anecdote or a thought for life, something to bring them back internally. People will only remember it if there is an emotion attached to it, so I try as much as possible to evoke an emotional response, whether that is joy, or pain, or fear, or whatever... and I do that with my slides. There will be a quote that is appropriate to a particular subject I'm talking about.

The outline is cut and dried, but when I need to go internally or emotionally, I have a slide that does that. It is more pictorial, and it draws in those people who may have gone to their happy place, mentally, because what I am talking about is not the most exciting thing, but you can bring them back emotionally by giving them something to think about and go "hmmm" or "wow, that strikes a note with me." I see people taking pictures of those slides. Actually, I give people an outline for notes, but they clearly take pictures to supplement what they respond to.

Once we've added in multi-sensory stories, our brain needs to know where to store everything we are taking in. We need a central idea tied to each piece of information or assertion or emotion. The solution is to provide your audience with a clear overall map of your lecture and guideposts along the way. The big picture of the map is the why. Why is this important to me and how will it serve me? Next, break down the steps of how to accomplish the task or use the new information. As you transition from step to step, put in a subheading slide that either ties back to the why or shows the progress along the journey. Finally, truly successful talks end with a clear call to action. Once again, highlight the why, show the steps in their entirety, and give the audience an easy and memorable path forward.

## How to Change Behavior

In addition to dealing with short-term versus long-term memory, we are also trying to drive behavior. As we learned from Simon Sinek's "Start with Why" talk, humans don't connect to data, to research findings, or to charts. We connect to people and their stories. Stories help us relate, make us feel, and provide our memories with context for learning and storing new ideas.

In crafting your presentation, think about the central problem you are solving, the point of pain you initially struggled with. Was there a patient you couldn't help? Or a procedure that failed? Were you pushing the proverbial rock up the hill in your business? What did you do? How did you feel? Tell the version of the story that includes your fears and frustrations.

This level of intimacy engages people in being open to hearing more. Instead of having arms crossed because they are being told something, they are leaning forward to listen more intently. Now you can share the story associated with the discovery of the solution. Was it your own research? Did someone help point the way? Can you share the trial and error process? Perhaps you can share some funny detours along the way. Data are important here because they give the audience assurances that this solution has been tested in real-life situations.

Finally, tell about the moment you realized that you had found the solution to your problem, that "aha" moment. Project your enthusiasm and hold the torch high. This story can be about the original scenario or case studies that are most relevant to your current success.

# Adult Learning Principles

Like it or not, we must contend with stubborn and judgmental people in our audience. New ideas often bring out our aversion to change, suspicion, or a jaded attitude. As such, it is helpful to understand how adults learn best and what presentation strategies we can employ to drive new behavior.

Here are some adult learning principles and strategies for our presentations:

### *I must choose to learn.*

Your audience may not engage if they don't perceive that they are currently experiencing a problem. Ask the audience to consider the last time they had a patient who presented the particular clinical challenge under discussion. Was the treatment path clear and the outcome successful? Are they open to considering a different method of treatment? In addition, ask them if they have constantly been running up against the same difficulty with a task and if they are open to trying a new way of handling it that has worked for you.

These opening questions engage the learner in a more personal manner and help diffuse the ingrained suspicion of being sold.

### *I'll only change if I want to.*

A good presentation will detail multiple options with pros and cons for each. A great presenter will offer stories associated with their experience with each of those options as a means of gaining credibility for their ultimate recommendation. This method provides the adult learner with responsibility for their decisions while also providing the expertise of the speaker as an element for consideration.

## *How is this different?*

While children are handed knowledge to assimilate, adults weigh new information against what they already know. Many times, people quickly discard information when they think, "I've already tried that and it didn't work" or "That won't work in my situation." A presenter needs to address these assumptions up front and delineate how their recommendation should be perceived against likely prior experience. Alternatively, the speaker can address their own initial reaction to the new option and discuss their personal pathway to adoption and ultimate success.

## *Why do I care?*

Most of the audience is at least interested enough in the topic to invest their time and/or money to be there. Capitalize on that and jump early and often into case studies or real-life examples. Perhaps there was a particular situation that was the catalyst for change. Use that story to craft the entire presentation, weaving the story into each stage of the journey. Pepper other stories into the presentation as a way to humanize data and engage the audience in relating to your message.

## *I'll only remember if I need it.*

There will be those in the audience whose primary need are CE credits or whose attendance is mandatory. By utilizing the above techniques, there is an increased likelihood that more of the attendees will walk away having not only learned something new but also having gained a willingness to implement change.

By spending the time to think about storytelling and focusing on a central purpose and adult learning principles, you will have a compelling and memorable lecture that will delight your audiences!

# CHAPTER 10
## TYING DESIGN TO YOUR SPEAKER STYLE, AUDIENCE, AND VENUE

Now it is time to put all of these design aspects together to create slides that will support your speaking goal and help the audience learn your material. There are three primary lenses I use when considering slide design; speaker style, audience communication style and venue elements.

# PRIORITY 1: DESIGN IN HARMONY WITH YOUR SPEAKER STYLE.

I've heard it said, "Leave funny to the funny people," and "Embrace your genius because that is where you will find the greatest success." What I take this to mean is don't try to be someone you aren't. I know I am not particularly funny, so I don't try to build in lots of jokes in my talks. I am however very passionate about what I believe in, and I think that comes through when I speak.

I also think how we dress, how we walk on stage, and what slides or props we use should be in harmony with who we are. Jim Carrey and Bill Gates would not dress the same nor use the same type of visual aids. Once we know our style, we should do everything to support our main purpose for speaking in the first place.

Each speaker style (Chapter 2) has a design style that harmonizes with its purpose. We should use fonts, colors, and images to further our overall messaging.

## Speaker Style Review:

 The recruiter has a product/service that they believe will benefit their audience.

 The inspirer excels in their field and wants to move the audience forward.

 The teacher has a love for their profession and wants to pay it forward.

 The informer has new information that the audience needs to be successful.

# Recruiter

The recruiter's communication style is direct and to the point. Their natural style is to be modern and to present credible information in a professional manner. In addition, if the audience knows in advance that this is the style of lecture they are attending, they will want to know how well this has worked for others. The recruiter should include lots of case studies and concrete examples so that the audience can relate to the beginning, understand how things will be done during the process, and recognize what they can hope to attain.

MODERN
CREDIBLE
PROFESSIONAL

THE RECRUITER'S GOAL:
For people to see the value of
their systems/products.

The recruiter would do well to use:

**POWER COLORS:** RED is an action color, so it suits them well. They also like the clarity of blacks and whites.

**STRONG FONTS:** Bolded San Serif (e.g., Avenir Family, Futura, Century Gothic).

**IMPACTFUL IMAGES:** Icons, clear blocks of information, and isolated images (without busy backgrounds).

## Cost Savings and Efficiency

**Conventional Chair-Side Conversion**

1) Records: Preliminary /Final Impressions etc.
2) Bite Reg. or Wax Try-in of Missing Teeth
3) Chair-side Conversion of Immediate Denture to Temporary Fixed Hybrid
4) Records: Abutment Level Impressions etc.
5) Screw Retained Bite Block, V-Jig Try-in
6) Screw Retained Try-in with Teeth in Wax
7) Delivery of Final Prosthesis

**Guided Prosthetics®**

1) Records: Fantastic Five
2) Guided Implant Surgery/LTP//Clear Duplicate
3) Tooth Try-In with Titanium Milled Bar
4) Delivery of the Final Prosthesis

*A clean visual layout drives the message home*

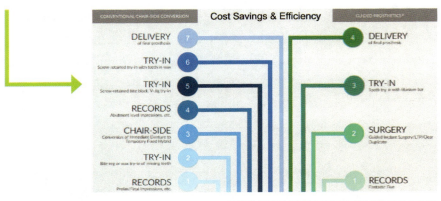

USED WITH PERMISSION BY DR IAN AIRES

## Inspirer

The inspirer's communication style is bold and enthusiastic. Their natural style is to be a storyteller. They love to entertain, and whether that is through passion or humor, you know you will go on a journey with them. They are typically at the top of their field and use speaking as a way to show others what's possible. They know that their audience won't be able to achieve the same results, but their hope is that some will grow and stretch. However, don't forget to include at least a few pearls that they can use themselves. The inspirer should expect that the audience wants to be wowed and not shy away from showing their very best.

The inspirer wants to engage people with enthusiasm and energy, so they should use:

**BRIGHT COLORS:** Reds, oranges, and yellows/gold.

**BOLD or HANDRAWN FONTS:** Some speakers will also use a mix of a few fonts to catch your eye.

**FULL-SCREEN PHOTOS:** Images that make you feel something. They could be personal, inspirational, surprising, or funny.

*Color, image and font combine for two very different types of inspirers*

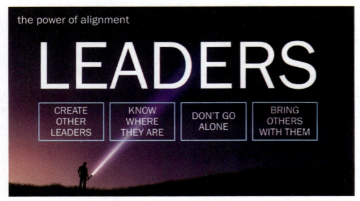

USED WITH PERMISSION BY BOB SPIEL

USED WITH PERMISSION BY DEBRA ENGELHARDT-NASH

# Teacher

The teacher's communication style is very friendly and casual. Their natural style is to want to get to know the audience and ask lots of questions. The teacher should include lots of step-by-step instructions, images, and if possible, hands-on exercises so that the audience will actually learn to do the procedure that they are being taught.

The teacher's goal is to help others feel comfortable learning something new, so they do well with:

CASUAL
FRIENDLY
PERSONAL

THE TEACHER'S GOAL:
To teach others how to do
something for a better end result.

**MUTED COLORS:** Greens (promote serenity), blues (convey a sense of trust), magenta/pink, and browns.

**SOFTER, FRIENDLY FONTS:** Helvetica Family, Cooper, Mistral, Blend of San Serif and Serif.

**STORYTELLING IMAGES:** Personal photos, allegorical images, and realistic icons.

## Review

**Clinical**

Long history of variable discomfort

Pain is usually mild to moderate

Pain on biting, "bad taste"

Symptoms don't settle after RCT

Deep narrow probing depth

Mid root swelling

sharp cracking sound

**Radiographic**

Isolated horizontal bone loss

Bifurcation bone loss

Radiolucent halos

V-shaped diffuse bone loss

Widened PDL

J-shaped bone loss

Fracture lines along the root

Space beside a root filling or post

Step-like bone defects

*Checklist image and muted design elicits trust and confidence*

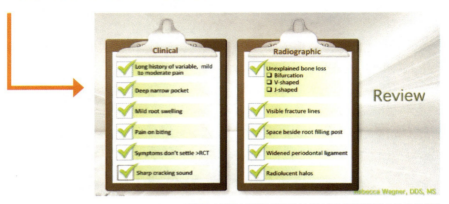

USED WITH PERMISSION BY DR REBECCA WAGNER

 **Informer**

The informer's communication style is typically quite conservative and analytical. Their natural style is a bit formal, and they approach speaking as a chance to share all the information that they think is important (which is all of it). They expect others to be as riveted by all these details as they are. The informer should provide data in easy-to-read formats (charts, graphs or diagrams, or images) so that the audience will gain both a high-level conclusion as well as proof of each point made.

The informer wants to transmit information in a clear and concise manner, so they would do best with:

**CLEAN, CONSERVATIVE COLORS:** blues/turquoise, black, white, and grays.

**TRADITIONAL SERIF FONTS:** Arial, Gill Sans, Times New Roman, and Constantia.

**VISUAL IMAGES:** Icons, charts, and diagrams that increase comprehension.

*Clean design, conservative colors and visual icons help transmit the message*

USED WITH PERMISSION BY GRACE RIZZA

The same content can and should be laid out in harmony with who you are and what you want to accomplish.

## Here is an example of the same bullet-style slides designed four different ways:

USED WITH PERMISSION BY LINDA MILES

# PRIORITY 2: ADAPT YOUR DESIGN TO ALIGN WITH YOUR AUDIENCE'S COMMUNICATION STYLES

Just as there are the four different speaker styles that are tied to our driving purpose for speaking, there are distinct ways people like to receive their information. Remember, although we should align our talks with our strengths, we are NOT the hero of the day, our audience is.

As such, we need to know more about our heroes in order to give them what they need. One of the ways we can do this is to understand that there are various communication styles that have been categorized by various researchers. I think one of the easiest to remember is the DISC Communication Style method.

## D  The Dominant/Driver style (D)

is the more outgoing and task-oriented person. They like to get things done without lots of drawn-out discussion. These are your classic Type A personalities. They want you to be brief, be brilliant, and be gone. They will be wowed by your ability to use every moment effectively and give them the big picture immediately.

> When designing for a D audience, I use declarative sentences, power colors, a clean strong font, and simple icons that will give a strong, simple get-to-the-point message.

## The Influencer/Expressive style (I)

is outgoing and people-oriented. The social butterfly. They love fun, new ideas, and to be in on the latest trends. You will find success with an "I" if you take a more personal approach and name drop whenever possible. Don't give them lots of details and instead focus on the big picture.

The I's in the audience will appreciate bright, cheerful, and fun slides. You can achieve this with deliberate choices—from the background to your fonts to the images you use. However, make sure you are also giving them immediate answers to their needs without lots of fuss.

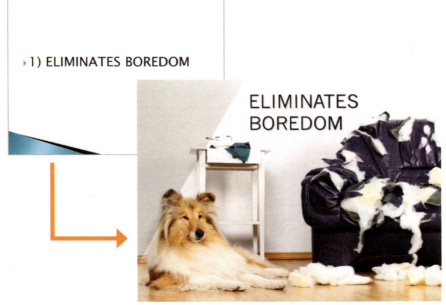

USED WITH PERMISSION BY LINDA MILES

# S

## The Supportive/Steadiness style (S)

is more reserved and people-oriented. They make sure everyone else is fine and can't stand conflict. Decision-making is one of their greatest challenges, so they will need your help working through things to determine which choice is best for them. It's not about having the newest or best with the S types. Safety, security, and family matter more to them.

If I were teaching a group of mostly S's, I would start out telling a story and show an image of people easily doing the new procedure or task. I would frequently add slides with affirmations and/or testimonials. In addition, I would use greens and blues in my design to give the sense of peace and security. I would probably choose a well-known font family such as Helvetica because a sense of familiarity is important when S's are learning new concepts.

*Use photos that feel good to deliver the message*

## C Finally, the Compliant/Conscientious style (C)

is reserved and task-oriented. They love facts, figures, graphs, and research. They will want a thorough analysis of new concepts and need time to come to any new conclusions. The C would rather avoid anything too personal or touchy-feely.

The C's in the audience like clean, organized spaces, so my slide design would match that—not too much clutter, very simple boxes for text, and easy-to-read data diagrams with references for them to check out later. I would stick to primary colors such as black, white, blue, and possibly a muted red or green. I would also use a singular San Serif font for additional readability and simplicity.

*While this is good...*

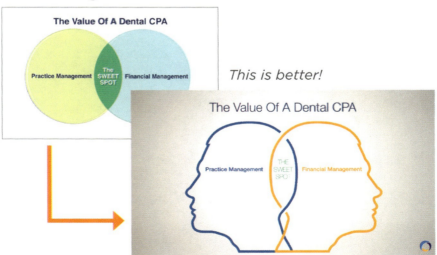

*This is better!*

USED WITH PERMISSION BY HADEN WERHAN

If you know these communication styles, you can quickly guess what someone is and adjust your conversation to deliver what they are most comfortable with. However, what do we do with an audience we don't know?

Reports on the general population breakdown of DISC styles vary due to the scoring systems used by different companies. Wiley, for instance, is one of the leading companies who administrates the DISC test, but their algorithm normalizes the data to ensure an even distribution of each communication style. The following chart illustrates this distribution.

| | | | |
|---|---|---|---|
| DC | 7.5% | | |
| D | 8.8% | } 24.8 | D |
| Di | 8.5% | | |
| iD | 7.1% | | |
| i | 10.4% | } 25.1 | i |
| iS | 7.6% | | |
| Si | 8.4% | | |
| S | 9.2% | } 25.7 | S |
| SC | 8.1% | | |
| CS | 9.9% | | |
| C | 9.2% | } 24.4 | C |
| CD | 5.3% | | |

https://www.discprofile.com/resources-and-tools/faq/

However, I did find a company who did a global research project using over 300,000 respondents in over 90 countries. They intentionally didn't normalize the data to see what variances they might uncover. The next figure demonstrates the distribution for various countries.

http://ttisuccessinsights.com/wp-content/uploads/2016/04/intl_norming_white_paper.pdf

# BASED UPON THIS, THE MAJORITY (~70%) OF THE US GENERAL POPULATION IS LIKELY TO BE AN I OR S STYLE.

However, we can make some stereotypical assumptions if our audience is made up of certain professions. Here are some typical jobs that could align with each style:

**D: Business owner/manager, sales, leader, project manager.**

**I: Trainer/teacher, sales, office manager, reporter, public relations/marketing.**

**S: Health care professional, human resources, team member.**

**C: Accountant, analyst, researcher, health care professional, programmer, engineer.**

Thus, if we are giving a lecture to accountants, we would want to give lots of details and stay away from long, drawn-out stories. On the other hand, if we are presenting a talk on marketing, we would want to include lots of fun and stay away from a deep dive into an analysis of the data.

Given that many dental practitioners are precise and analytical, we might assume that they tend towards the C style. In addition, both dentists and their team members chose healthcare because they want to help people, so there are likely many with the S style.

At the end of the day, we can only make an educated guess. If the audience is likely to be a true blend, I recommend designing solely with your own speaker style in mind, but if we think our audience will be more homogenous to one communication style, why wouldn't we want to deliver our information in the way that they like to receive it?

# Venue Considerations for Designing Your Slides

The three elements that you need to know before you design your slides are the dimensions of the screen, the meeting room size and how the room will be lit.

### Screen Dimension / Aspect Ratio

There are three standard screen sizes:

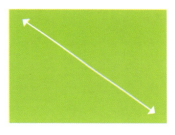 4:3 is almost square. This was the standard for the past couple of decades. Almost all portable pop-up screens are this size, and many smaller venues only have this capability.

 16:9 is rectangular and was introduced over the past decade as widescreen TVs became more mainstream.

 3:1 is a super-wide rectangle and is sometime used at larger symposiums (more frequently in Europe).

### Which aspect ratio should I use?

If you are developing a talk for a particular program, ASK the venue what screen size they will have. If you have a choice, or will be using this talk at multiple venues, I recommend using 16:9. In my opinion, the 4:3 slides seem old-school, sort of like the old square TV box. In addition, you can easily display 16:9 slides on a flatscreen TV and/ or a computer screen. The 16:9 slides even look good on a square screen, they just display with a blank space above and below the slides. From a design perspective, the larger rectangular space lends itself to a cleaner layout with plenty of breathing room.

A word of caution: only use 3:1 if you will be presenting on that specific screen size. If you try to display it on a 16:9 screen size, it will display very thin across the standard-size screens, and your text and images will be smaller than you had hoped.

## Room Size Drives Font Sizes

Don't forget that your font size needs to be easily read by the person in the last row. There aren't any hard and fast rules, but I use these guidelines in my design:

1. Meeting rooms (fewer than 12 people): Fonts should be no smaller than 20 pt. (12 pt. for references or ancillary data).

2. Seminars (fewer than 50 people): Fonts should be no smaller than 24 pt. (16 for references or ancillary data).

3. Keynote presentations (auditoriums or halls): Fonts should be 40–90 pt. (24 for references or ancillary data).

One way to ensure success without having to worry about font size is the squint test. While you are designing each slide, if you squint to the point where the font gets fuzzy, can you still tell the purpose of that slide? If not, redesign it.

## Lighting Affects Background Color Choice

There are three background color choices: Dark, light, and mixed/medium.

## Which background color should I use?

The rule of thumb is
**the darker the room, the darker the background,**

*Images and font pop here*          *and are washed out here*

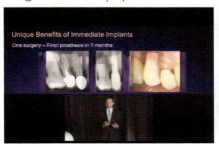 

and the lighter the room, the lighter the background.

*Images and font pop here*          *and are washed out here*

If you use the same presentation in a variety of settings, I recommend using a moderate, neutral-toned background based upon your speaker style colors.

Changing over your background is very easy in PowerPoint. The fastest way is to click on the Design tab, select Format Background, and once you have picked what you like, click on Apply to All at the bottom.

# THE WINNERS' ROUNDTABLE

# CHAPTER 11
## SPEAKER TIPS

One of my goals with this book was to share nuggets that I gleaned from the very generous speakers who have contributed to this book. Three areas I asked them to share about include time management tips, lessons they have learned along the way, and advice that they would like to pass along.

## QUESTION

How have you dealt with **time management** challenges as a speaker?

### LINDA MILES

I had to decide what I am best at so that I could stop trying to do everything. It turns out that I am best on the phone or in front of an audience speaking to people and getting them excited about their careers. I am NOT good at making travel arrangements, working out nitty-gritty details with the meeting planners, and so forth. As a result, I hired the best person to do these tasks for me. I honestly believe that 50% of my re-bookings were because meeting planners loved working with my Executive Director, Lee Tarvin. So many planners are busy traveling, which makes them difficult to work with. Lee was organized, sent them what they needed by the due dates, and was always kind; plus, she remembered them by name from previous conversations. She also sent cards, little gifts, and developed relationships with them.

## DR. ROY SHELBURNE

For me, it's just like a dental practice; you can systematize everything. I don't have an assistant, so after a presentation, I offer the attendees something I call a tool box. It's all prepackaged, so once I get their emails, I can just fire that off. Anything I do more than once or twice, I develop a system for, so it becomes very easy for me to execute.

When someone contacts me for a speaking or consulting engagement, I have a set of materials I send, a timeline that I use for following up, and so forth. Having systems doesn't mean it always works perfectly, but it gives me a way to measure what is working and what isn't, and then I can change the systems as needed. Even as specific as looking at people of different age groups and looking at what they need to be able to make decisions... it's kind of interesting; it's always great to be able to figure out who is the ultimate decision maker and figure out how you can communicate with that person, find out something about that person so you have the information you need to be able to provide them with the tools they need to be able to make an appropriate decision.

## DR. TANYA BROWN

Finding a good work-life balance is important, because speaking and travel can be seductive and time consuming. Everyone has 24 hours in a day, and how we choose to use that time is what makes a difference. Focus on the things that resonate with you, and that you have a natural talent for. Then, create an outline, goals, and framework. That saves me a lot of time. I have also worked with several professional speaking coaches who have shortened my learning curve. I also now work with Margy Schaller to create the slides and handouts from my framework. It used to take me forever and is never as good as using someone who does this all the time. That is a HUGE time saver.

## DR. STEVEN SADOWSKY

Time is the most precious thing we have. My family says I don't need to put as much time into preparation because they think I am experienced enough do a good job, but I still feel compelled to invest long hours into each new project. However, it has helped to have a compendium of slides on various topics and a familiarity with pertinent subtopics so that I can be more efficient in reformatting a presentation.

## RACHEL WALL, RHD

I use checklists as I'm prepping to leave for a speaking gig. I have all the things I need to bring—slide changer, mac adapter, batteries, and so forth— all in a small zippered bag so that I can grab it quickly when I am packing. I have my notes for each speech in a clear sleeve so that I don't have to re-create it every time, and I can add to it as I learn.

I share a lot of resources with my audience, so now I am working on streamlining processes to get that done.

## DR. JOEL ROSENLICHT

It always seems to be a very time-consuming process for all these lectures. For every hour of lecture, it's like five hours of preparation. You have to dedicate the time to do it well (unless you are giving a canned presentation over and over again...), which I don't seem to have the luxury of doing.

The more I do this, in a way it is easier, but in a way, it's a lot harder. I don't know if this is because I put more pressure on myself, but I think sometimes I am able to look at these presentations with a bit more ease because I can use much of my previous content and just update, refresh, and/or rearrange based upon the requests. I am very conscious that I have to be careful about speaking too much on the same content to the same people.

## DR. TIM SILEGY

The most time-consuming part of presentation development is finding representative cases and organizing them in a way that helps you make your point. A presentation designer can help you with the final product, but only you can choose what you want to present.

For me, the most challenging part is downloading pictures from the camera, getting them organized in some fashion, and even remembering what I have. I have so many excellent surgical cases where I didn't get the final photos from the restorative dentist, and now I don't have that complete case. Try to have the organizational systems and discipline to follow through with them in place.

What **lessons** have you learned along the way?

**DR. STEVEN SADOWSKY**

I joined a number of prosthodontics societies, and for some of these, you had to make a presentation to join, and that is where some of the honing of my skills happened because their standards were so high. A simple presentation wasn't going to be good enough, so this helped me raise the bar, and after that, I was able to see some inspirational and creative presentations that delivered some very potent conclusions. Seeing what it should look like... that helped a lot. However, I learned that I had to place my own insignia on my presentations. For me, it was capturing the attention of the audience with sometimes surprising premises and supporting them with robust evidence. Carl Sagan once said, "Extraordinary claims require extraordinary evidence." To capture the imagination of the attendees and offer them unexpected practical tools in their arsenal of treating their patients have been reliable keys to my success as a speaker. Last, adding anecdotes about my clinical experience, especially the errors, offers an instructive element and a more intimate window into me as the speaker.

## DR. ROY SHELBURNE

I always venerated people who were speakers, and having become part of that network, I truly understand that speakers are very intelligent, but they're just folks like you and me. They may or may not practice every day, but they are normal folks with a passion and a desire to share what they know with an industry that could benefit from that knowledge. I had a different view of speakers and who they were and what they represented, so that was surprising. Now, if there is something that is vexing or confusing to me, I'll reach out to one of my peers and ask them. I've been blessed to have had good fortune with speaking thus far, but I've not been doing it for very many years, and I'm confident that I don't know half of the things that people who have been in it for decades know.

These speakers really do care about individual people, and it's not a detached kind of thing for them. The best speakers in the country are the ones that DO develop that connection and that one-to-one interaction. They have a very specific desire to benefit everyone who attended that seminar. I had no idea how engaged these speakers are in the lives of the people who attend seminars and lectures.

## DR. TIM SILEGY

In my profession, it's very difficult to get on the speaker circuit. Once you are on, it's a good ride, but it comes with a cost. Unless speaking will be your primary source of income, which for me it is not, you'll have to balance your personal and professional life. It's very easy to get caught up with the glamour of being a speaker. Truth be told, it's a bit of a grind to be traveling all the time.

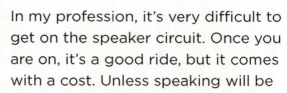

## DR. JOEL ROSENLICHT

I gave up a LOT to chase my ambitions. Early in my career, I lived dentistry, oral surgery, and implants almost 100% of the time, so much so that it did affect my personal life. I was away a lot, I was traveling on the weekends, I was working evenings, and we had two young children at that time who I think were getting a little neglected. I think making sure you balance a lifestyle with work is important because it's so easy to get wrapped up in it that it can be an overwhelming part of your life.

Later in my career, I had another choice to make. I don't know if this was the right or wrong thing to have done, but when I became president of various organizations, I felt that there was a conflict of interest to continue to be involved with industry and still do lectures. I know that there have been a lot of people in the same positions who did not stop doing these activities, but I did. That was a significant detour for my speaking career, but I was very busy with the administrative duties of those roles, and you can only do so much.

Once I returned to speaking, I was able to pick it back up and keep going, but I had lost a lot of ground. There is a momentum that you get when you are a relatively active speaker on the circuit, and when you drop off the scene for a while, it's a little harder to get back because people aren't aware of who you are anymore. You are only as good as you are at the times that you are speaking.

### DR. TOM KEPIC

My life balance is non-existent. I've literally given up my life for my profession—not kidding at all. I've suffered through two divorces, including all the difficult court proceedings around those divorces. Also, I was a single parent for my son from age 4½ to 16½. I would sit with him on the sofa while putting my lectures together, and he was my audience as I practiced. He is now 26 and a joy in my life.

I wish now that I had known Margy Schaller a long time ago. I've sat through many hundreds of lectures and could never figure out how the speakers could ever put together their presentations with all the arrows, circles, fade-ins, and more. Not only would knowing that have saved me hours of my time, but I think I could have been a better presenter.

## DR. ROY SHELBURNE

Regardless of who I'm speaking to, I value their time and who they are personally. "No" is not no, it's more than likely "Not now." Never burn a bridge or do anything that you would not want done to you. Most importantly, be easy to work with. Work at being the easiest speaker they've ever worked with, and in this small industry, people will talk. Under-promise and over-deliver.

## LINDA MILES

At my peak, for 12 years (1987–1999), I was on the road 200 days a year; I had six other consultants and nine other people working at my corporate office. I was making a ton of money (~$150,000/month), but I was killing myself slowly. When you have a big office and lots of employees, you have to work really hard to feed that animal. This is not a glamorous life, and it's not easy. It is very, very hard work.

TIP: Keep your business LEAN and CLEAN! Outsource that which you are not good at or don't have time to do. Keep your overhead low. It is not what you produce that measures success but what you keep as net profit each year.

On a speaking assignment, typically the evening before, the host wants to take you to dinner. Many times over the years I went because I enjoyed learning about their group, but oftentimes, later in my travels, I preferred to stay in my hotel room, have room service, and go to sleep early. Therefore, I learned to graciously decline their offer. I may have been in three previous cities within three days... Calling my family and resting was much more fun than being entertained.

**QUESTION**

What **advice** would you be willing to pass along to other speakers?

## DR. STEVEN SADOWSKY

That's simple. What is a speaker passionate about? I realized that speaking is a road to finding our own creativity. It also continues to reveal how to become more effective as a communicator. It is a gift to be part of this ongoing process.

You need to believe in yourself and know that you have something unique to offer (versus comparing yourself to others and seeing what's missing or lacking) and begin to appreciate that your perspective may be the foundation for a dynamic approach.

It's important to personalize your lectures and to include personal stories. People want to connect and have a relationship with you as a speaker. I think that if we don't do this, there is an invisible shield and people become disenfranchised. Martin Buber called this forging an I-Thou rather than an I-It relationship.

## DR. ROY SHELBURNE

The greatest myth is that you can't do this. You absolutely can! Anybody can do it if they have (1) the passion; (2) the ability (which can be learned); and (3) the energy, effort, and commitment to make it happen. A lot of people think that this all happens organically, but it's a lot of work. However, if people think it's been easy for you, you are doing it right because no meeting planner or client wants to hire someone who is desperate.

First off, unless and until you have confidence in your presentation and your skills, don't do it, or do this for no money for people who are not going to develop your reputation for you. It's like anything else, you are only as good as your last presentation. I'm a CE junkie, so I attend other presentations to see how I can raise my own bar. The people who are busy speaking are great speakers. You can't be a mediocre speaker with great information and be successful. You are going to have to have both skill and some charisma to be able to make it work, and that charisma comes from passion, and people are drawn to passionate people. If you love what you do, some of it will wear off on to them.

## DR. TOM KEPIC

I would seek out both a speaking coach and presentation consultant/ designer. The coach has already been down the road several times and will already know what you don't even know and will help ask the necessary questions on what it is that you are trying to accomplish.

Get clarity on the topic, the content selection, and how you are going to go about getting the information out. Before you start putting in the clinical slides, doing a literature search, reading journals, and putting it into PPT, sit down with a professional and create your presentation from the inside-out, not from the outside in.

Form follows function—it's like building a house, the form should follow the function of the house. The same thing goes with public speaking. Build the presentation from within, and then all the rest will come naturally. The frosting and cake decorations are NOT the cake itself. The real thing is that you are there to eat the cake, and you could miss the whole opportunity by designing it from the outside in. It's the cake that you are really after.

**LINDA MILES**

Join the NSA or Dale Carnegie, and if you are serious about being a speaker in dentistry, you should join SCN, where likeminded dental speakers, consultants, and authors meet with meeting planners who hire speakers, dental companies that have products or services their clients can use to make practices better, and editors from leading dental journals who need writers. Network with the people you feel are your competitors. Academy of Dental Management Consultants (ADMC) is also a group mostly for consultants. I believe that if you embrace your competition, everyone wins. The scarcity notion never works. If you share how you grow your business with 10 others and learn from them, everyone will grow, and everyone's clients will benefit from the shared knowledge.

**RACHEL WALL, RHD**

Be real. Be yourself. Admit when you are struggling with something. I get feedback from people who say that they feel I'm real and approachable.

Invest in working with experts to help accelerate your own growth and development because it will take a lot longer to grow if you are just relying on yourself.

### DR. TANYA BROWN

Take it seriously and be open to learning. Treat this as a business- it is. I am a practicing dentist, so I must be willing to double down on my schedule when I have a lecture:

**Sun,** 12 hrs preparing
**Mon,** 8 hrs patients, practice my lecture at night 2 hrs
**Tues,** 8 hrs patients
**Wed,** 4 hrs patients, drive/fly to location and have dinner with organizers
**Thurs,** 4-6 hrs Lecture, drive/fly home
**Fri,** 8 hrs office work

The quote, "When you are interested in something, you will do what is convenient. But when you are committed to something, you will do whatever it takes." resonates with me. This means putting in the hours, practicing, setting yourself aside to focus on the audience, and perfecting your skills.

## DR. TIM SILEGY

Be honest. Don't sugarcoat how you feel on a given topic. Also, be humble. I tell my audiences, "I'm not better than any other oral and maxillofacial surgeon. I just have an interest in helping others be successful."

Talk into people's listening; otherwise, you are like the teacher in the Charlie Brown cartoon, unseen and unheard. The key to being a good speaker is keeping the audience's attention and giving participants something tangible that they can use afterwards.

## LINDA MILES

Be original. Don't read a good book and regurgitate it to people who may have also read the same book! If you quote someone, give them credit.

Zig Ziglar used to say, "When someone steals my material the first time, they say, 'as Zig Ziglar says...,' and the second time they say, 'as some people say...,' and the third time, they say, 'as I always say....'" So, make sure it's your material or credit the source!

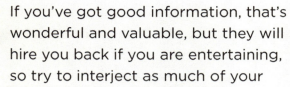

### DR. ROY SHELBURNE

If you've got good information, that's wonderful and valuable, but they will hire you back if you are entertaining, so try to interject as much of your personality and humor as you can. People won't remember everything you said, but they will remember how you made them feel. If I can make them feel a little bit better about who they are and what they are doing and also give them tools to do better, then that's magic.

### DR. TANYA BROWN

I have found that the more I can bring my authentic self to each program, the more I get booked, so I put my attention there instead of chasing that next gig.

### DR. TIM SILEGY

I've noticed that time has become a more valuable commodity for people, so I think a successful speaker today needs to be able to deliver a strong message in a shorter amount of time. The idea of people spending all day at a course listening to someone go "blah blah blah" is old. I don't think people want to do that anymore, so be ready to do evening programs or shorter programs. Some of the bigger meetings are now scheduling programs where speakers just roll one after the other with 15-20 minute sessions so the audience can get a selection of great ideas.

## DR. STEVEN SADOWSKY

The New York Times had an Op Ed article that said that intelligence is not a predictor of success, but rather grit, diligence, conscientiousness, openness, and curiosity are, and those are things we can change and improve. I think it is so important that we can experience the depth of our powerful compact of assets, and if we have made mistakes along the way, that is good because we can perfect our techniques. So much emphasis has been placed upon testing and results but not on celebrating the learning along the way that leads to true empowerment. Public speaking is the passageway to follow this process. Refinement, confidence, and compassion are the natural outcomes of this sustained work. It is way to make a difference for both the audience and the speaker.

## LINDA MILES

I never pretend to know something I don't know, but I constantly read all the dental journals and newsletters to stay current. However, there are certain areas of sub-specialties (insurance coding, legal, HR, etc.), that I won't touch anymore because the details are so different and change too fast. I just stay current with my areas of expertise and make sure that I know the best consultants to refer people to for the other topics.

What I do is to refresh and readdress my material. I have had people who have been listening to me for 24 years who say that they always learn something new, partially because my material is timeless and people learn what they need to at that time in their lives.

Zig Ziglar and Nido Qubein were great mentors of mine, and while you may not remember what the seminar was about, we all remember the stories. I use a lot of humor, and I learned from Zig that "you don't have to use humor unless you want to be invited back and paid," so I learned to be real funny, real fast. The stories all come from my life— things that may not have been funny at the time but over time grew to be. I keep a journal of these things to use in my lectures.

## DR. JOEL ROSENLICHT

You really need to get comfortable speaking in a way that can identify with your audience. They can sense when you are not comfortable, or not "on," and you need to give them the best that you can. In a way, you are performing a little bit; you are exposing yourself to criticism, so be honest with yourself and your audience and enjoy what you are doing.

It's been a great opportunity. The speaking and the people that I have met over the past 37 years have really made my career go very quickly. I think we are really fortunate in dentistry to have the opportunity to do so many different things for our patients, for ourselves, and for our profession.

# CHAPTER 12
## THE FORMULA FOR A WINNING PRESENTATION

I wrote this book for you, the hero of the story. I am here as the guide, providing you with the tools for you to conquer your Mount Everest. As I said in the beginning, whether you found a nugget or a new way of thinking, my goal is to help you write a compelling talk, design a memorable presentation and succeed with your speaking career.

Here is your step-by-step formula for a winning presentation.

## STEP 1
# UNCOVER YOUR WHY
Write down your inner heart's purpose for your presentation in a complete sentence.

## STEP 2
# IDENTIFY YOUR SPEAKER STYLE
Identify what speaker type you are for this program (recruiter, inspirer, teacher, informer) based upon what you hope the audience will do with your information.

## STEP 3
# DETERMINE YOUR BIG IDEA
Decide what one thing you want your audience to remember, your big idea. This should be in the form of a complete sentence that includes what's at stake for those who do or don't adopt your point of view.

## STEP 4
# BRAINSTORM YOUR TOPIC
Brainstorm and research your topic exhaustively without censure. Write each unique idea or fact on individual notecards.

## STEP 5
# SORT AND CHUNK YOUR NOTECARDS
Make logical stacks of your notecards, discarding those that are outliers. Move your stacks into some order (chronological, cause/effect, before/after).

## STEP 6
## EDIT FOR CLARITY
Discard any stack that doesn't absolutely support the big idea.

## STEP 7
## WRITE AN OUTLINE
Write your outline with clarity as the chief guide. Your audience doesn't want to know everything you know; they just want to know one thing they can use. Go deep rather than wide.

## STEP 8
## CHOOSE YOUR DESIGN STYLE
Use your speaker style, the typical audience make-up, and venue to determine your slide design style.

## STEP 9
## CREATE COMPELLING AND MEMORABLE SLIDES
Convert your outline to your presentation software (PowerPoint, Keynote, Prezi, etc.) and use your design style to apply colors, fonts, images and layout. Each slide and each word or image should only be there to clarify and drive home your one key message.

So there it is. Formulating a winning presentation starts with looking inside yourself and finding your passion, your purpose, and your message. That message needs to have utter clarity and be delivered in a harmonious manner that fulfills your audience's expectations and needs. Finally, create impact with visuals and storytelling that will make your message one that lasts past the exit door.

Thank you for allowing me to fulfill my why; to be of service in helping others become the best version of themselves. I invite you to take the next steps in fulfilling your why.

# Resources

Here is an easy access list of the resources I've provided throughout the book. This not meant to be a comprehensive list of the free design assets out there, rather as a starting place for you.

Simon Sinek Ted Talk "Start With Why"
- 5 min version:
  https://www.youtube.com/watch?v=IPYeCltXpxw
- Full version: https://www.ted.com/talks/simon_sinek_how_great_leaders_inspire_action

Brainstorming method
- "The Six Thinking Hats": http://sixthinkinghats.com

Fonts
- www.fontsquirrel.com
- www.fontspace.com

Color Palettes
- Color Scheme Designer:
  http://colorschemedesigner.com/csd-3.5/
- Popular palettes: www.colorlovers.com

Free images
- www.morguefile.com
- www.iconmonstr.com
- www.freeimages.com
- www.compfight.com

## About the Author

Margy Schaller is a presentation coach, designer, and speaker.  After obtaining her Instructional Design certification and working with speakers for 15 years, she launched her own firm, Laser Pointer in the summer of 2013.  As of December 2016, she has worked with almost 100 clients from not only the dental and medical space, but also legal, financial, real estate and renewable energy.  Laser Pointer is growing rapidly and adding team members to best support its primary mission:  To help each speaker become the best version of themselves.  To learn more, visit www.laserpointerpresentations.com

Margy lives in San Diego with her husband Bob, two Boston Terriers and a kitty.  Her daughter Megan and son-in-law Tom are nearby and they frequently enjoy game night together.  Megan and Margy also enjoy playing on a soccer team together.  Margy's son Rhett is graduating from San Jose State University in May 2017 and will be launching his career as a writer.  Her step-daughter Jessica is attending UCLA and is due to graduate in May 2018.

With the completion of this book, Margy hopes to return to her passions of gardening, arts and crafts, and watching football on a lazy Sunday.

# Acknowledgements

My first and biggest thanks goes to Stacy Reilly for co-designing this book with me. While I had a vision, and laid out my ideas, she took that and brought it to life. Stacy has her own presentation design business but we frequently work together on projects. It is an honor to have a colleague who is as good at her craft as Stacy is.

Next, I want to thank all the speakers who contributed to this book, not only those who I interviewed but also those who have shared their experiences and wisdom with me over the years. Linda Miles has been especially helpful by introducing me to the Speaking Consulting Network (SCN), and with all her encouragement throughout this journey. There were also 21 speakers who gave me permission to use their slides as examples. Thank you, thank you, thank you.

It is an honor and privilege that JoAn Majors was willing to write such a heartfelt foreword. JoAn was my first paying client when I launched my business. From Day One, she believed in me, even before I was sure if I could turn this business from a dream into a reality.

Thank you to my client and mentor Tonya Lanthier. Tonya (CEO of DentalPost.net) is one of the most inspirational business women I have ever met. She is warm, generous, crazy energetic, and has taught me more than she will ever realize. I don't know where my business would be without her encouragement, but I'm glad I didn't have to navigate this journey without her.

Thank you to Mark LeBlanc for sharing his wisdom and Henry DeVries for guiding me on how to shape my raw manuscript from a collection of thoughts into a focused book.

Thank you to my son Rhett Cookson.  He is launching his career as a writer and gave me the honest feedback I truly needed. It takes courage to tell someone you love that there is room for improvement, but he gifted me with his insight so I could produce this final product that I am so proud of.

And finally, my deepest gratitude goes to my husband Bob. For being unwavering in his support of every part of my business venture. For encouraging me to go for my dreams even though he had no idea whether it could be done. For supporting me as I wrote this book when I wasn't sure if I had the ability or stamina.  For telling me how proud he is that my hard work has converted into one success after another.

Made in the USA
Lexington, KY
17 January 2017